MINISTRY TO ALL NATIONS

Practical Theology of Mission and Church Planting

Dr. John G Githiga

SECOND EDITION

ISBN: 978-1-62217-511-6

OTHER BOOKS BY THE AUTHOR

The Spirit in the Black Soul
Christ and Roots
Initiation and Pastoral Psychology
The Secrets of Success in Marriage

About the Book

Ministry to All Nations is a dramatic story of how Bishop John and Rev. Mary Githiga went through fire without being burned. And how they used challenges as the stepping-stones to high achievements in ministry to All Nations. It is about their obedience to God regardless of the cost and about how to bear the cross so as to wear the crown. This is an ideal book for those who are being persecuted and those who are planting churches, starting new ministries, and venturing in missions.

About the author

Dr. Githiga is chancellor at ANCCI University. He was formerly chaplain and faculty at West Texas A&M University, Chaplain and faculty at Grambling State University, instructor at Pensacola Junior College, head of the Department of Pastoral Theology at St. Paul's University, and founder and first president of the African Association for Pastoral Study and Counseling. He is a graduate from Church Army College, St. Paul's United Theological College, Makerere University, the University of the South, Vanderbilt University, and the International Bible Institute and Seminary. He holds Dip.Th, M.Div, D.Min, DRE, and D.D. He is married to the Rev. Dr. Mary Githiga.

Acknowledgements

I am most grateful to Isaac Cyprian Githiga, Jerry Gill, and Bettye Wallace for proofreading this book, and to the bishops and ministers and evangelists of All Nations Christian Church International and the faculty and the students of ANCCI University. My hearty thanks also goes to Mama Mary Githiga for being a faithful companion and co-minister, and to our daughter, Rehema, for assisting with air tickets for our missionary journeys.

Table of Contents

INTRODUCTION

For over thirty years I have paid attention to my dreams. I have learned that, besides being the best means of individuation, meaning the communication between the conscious and the unconscious which enhances self-identity and increases the feeling of wholeness, dreams are telepathic and prophetic. When I was busy ministering as vicar/chaplain at the University Church and WTA&M University and venturing in mission to the African refugees and the recent immigrants from Mexico, I had a big dream. I saw myself in a beautiful white suit, visiting the refugees' neighborhood where I saw a double-faced toddler with male and female faces. He was alone. His/her faces looked like that of Deng and Abuk, children of the two families that I loved and visited quite often. Since the child was lying on his/her back naked, I was moved by compassion and stooped to pick him/her up. The toddler responded by directing his small tool at me and soaking my suit with urine. I still did not give up on him/her. I then bent down to reach him/her again. He then aimed at my head and soaked all of my hair with urine. I then woke up and found that it was a dream.

As you will see in this book, the dream was a prediction of the joy and pain that came from the ministry to the refugees and immigrants. We had unspeakable joy in ministering to the people who have suffered for their faith. They also freely accorded Mary and me respect and hospitality. Yet, there came a time when the hosting church was offended by the stinking suit. It was impossible to convince them that the urine was not mine, since I was the one wearing the suit. Besides, it was my hair that was stinking.

Nevertheless, whatever happens, God is in control and has our best interest at heart. God will allow us to go through Good Friday so as to enjoy Easter. For that reason we rejoice in our suffering, knowing that suffering produces endurance, endurance produces character, and character produces hope, and hope does not disappoint us, because God's love has been poured into our hearts through the Holy Spirit which has been given to us. Romans 5:3-5.

Before we enjoy eternal Easter, our loving Father will grant us the joy of many Easters. As I am writing this introduction, I couldn't believe what I saw in our master bedroom. The bed is covered with a golden comforter and cushions. It looks like heaven on earth. Guess who gave us these precious gifts. They came from Mabure and Amir, the parents of Deng who appeared in my dream four years ago. They had given us something that is more superior to the suit that I wore in the dream, even though I have never shared the dream with them. The gifts remind me that those who lose what they have for the sake of the Kingdom of God, their reward will be beyond human description. We have an inheritance that is imperishable, undefined, and unfading, kept in heaven for you, who by God's power are guarded through faith for a salvation ready to be revealed in the last time. I Peter 1:3-9

This book is a story of how God has used Mary and me to spearhead the ministry to all the people of God. It is also about so many saints who participated in throwing the spear through prayer. Our two mothers, Joyce Nyeri Githiga, and Joyce Wambui Kahungu interceded for us without ceasing. Canon Habel Gitogo Isaac, my elder brother, prays for us every day. There are also many prayer partners who pray with us and encourage us. Other people have given us financial support. We are most grateful to God, who gives us desire and will and energy and guidance and endurance. We glorify the Loving Father for letting us suffer various trials so that we may empathize with those who are suffering.

All glory to God.

It should also be mentioned that we do not use the actual names of the people who persecuted us. We have forgiven them and we wish them well. We are also convinced that one of the surprises in heaven will be to see some of those folks praising God with us, and to note that the seed, which we planted in tears, germinated and bore much fruit.

CHAPTER ONE:
AN ANSWER TO PRAYER

DOES GOD ANSWER THE PRAYER of the people? God indeed answers the prayer of the people. During the Lenten season of 2002, the Church, which I was ministering to using the Anglican Cycle of Prayer, prayed for three consecutive Sundays for the persecuted church in Sudan. On the third Sunday, I posed a question in the bulletin, "Did you know that for the last three Sundays we have been praying for the Episcopal Church in Sudan?" I then included a brief history of this persecuted church.

To my great surprise, during the week prior to this Sunday, I got a call from Deng saying, "We want to visit with you on Saturday."

"Who are we?" I asked.

"We are ten Sudanese families with thirty-one persons."

Deng was not new to us. Mary and I still remember how we met him in United Super Market and how Mary greeted him. "Are you from Sudan?"

"Yes, Mom," he responded.

We then took his telephone number and paid him a visit the following week.

So, when Deng called, Mary and I decided to invite those families on Saturday at 4:00 p.m. On that day Mary prepared the refreshments for thirty-one people. To our dismay, no one had arrived by 5:00 p.m.

When I called Deng's home, I was told that they had left at 4:00 p.m. to come to our home. At 6:30 p.m. there was a knock at the door. It was Deng and two other men. They apologized and told us that they were lost and that it was only through God's grace that they finally found our place.

As we took the refreshments, I asked them to tell their stories. They all had horror stories of how they fled from Sudan. Simon escaped from prison, where he was incarcerated for starting a Christian union at Khartoum University. He walked from Sudan to Cairo, Egypt.

After the dreadful stories they came to the point. "We have come to ask you to help us establish the African Community Church."

This was an unexpected request since it was seemingly out of season. I was already overstretched teaching at West Texas A&M University, ministering as chaplain, and engaging in heavy Lenten services at University Church. I felt as though I had no time or energy for planting a congregation. I recalled the time and energy I exerted when I was planting St. Nicholas' Church in Nakuru, Kenya. But I could not tell my Sudanese brothers, "Let me pray about it." We had already prayed and recorded our prayer in the church bulletin. Besides, I had already seen the vision of planting a church and shared the vision with the diocesan bishop. I then gave Deng and his friends the Sunday bulletin that made it plain that we have been praying for them. This situation was very much like Simon Peter and Cornelius who prayed and God revealed Himself to them in a vision. Both Simon Peter and Cornelius had to bridge cultural differences. Ministering with the Sudanese also entailed crossing another culture. They are Nilotic. I am a Bantu. They are from a pastoral tribe, I am from an agricultural tribe. They come from Arabic speaking Africa. I come from English speaking Africa. I am accustomed to ministering the professional, they are blue-collar workers.

Nevertheless, I perceived that God had sent them. I accepted their request to help them establish an African church. The Sunday bulletin, which recorded our prayers, made it plain that God had been preparing us for this mission. Being fully convinced by the Holy Spirit, I said to them, "This is not our mission, it is God's mission."

We then started discussing what God wanted us to do. I was so amazed by the way we agreed on many things within a short period of time. We agreed on the following:

We will establish a church, which will nurture, reconcile, and orient the African Christians to the American way of life.

The church will seek to become a mission of the Diocese of Northwest Texas.

We will use the Anglican liturgy and African Christian folk songs.

We will be worshiping at home.

Father Githiga will be the spiritual leader while Deng will be the chairman.

We will hold a meeting of all the members of the ten families on March 10, 2002, at 3:00 p.m. at Simon's home.

And the church will officially start on Palm/Passion Sunday, March 24, 2002.

Fourteen adults and fifteen children attended the first meeting. We started by hearing the stories of how the brothers and sisters fled from Sudan. Most of them had to go through three countries before they arrived in the United States. After sharing the stories, we then elected Simon as chairman, went through the Episcopal liturgy, decided that the worship would take place on Sunday at 6:15 p.m., and agreed that we will be singing in Arabic, Swahili, and English. And Mary was to teach women how to prepare American food. We then closed the meeting with prayer.

As we were driving home, Mary and I reflected on the stories and faces of the narrators. We perceived that they were wounded and that their wounds were still bleeding. And so we felt that they needed a healing service.

On the next Sunday we had a healing service. I anointed them with holy oil. The gloomy faces started glittering with joy. Mary taught them a new song: *REJOICE IN THE LORD ALWAYS* AND AGAIN I SAY REJOICE.

The congregation grew steadily. The members attracted other refugees. We now had people of God from several African countries and Mexico. Unity also brought Native Americans, African Americans, and European Americans. Within three months we had outgrown Deng's living room. Graciously, the Community of Grace United Methodist Church invited us to use their sanctuary. They had all the facilities we needed. To our greater surprise they asked us to pay only $25.00 per month for utilities and gave us a three-month grace period.

On July 7, 2002, we held our first Extravaganza to celebrate our first month in a church building and to express our gratitude to the Community of Grace. In Kenya, July 7 is known as saba saba (seven, seven). It symbolizes the birth of a multiparty political system, which was a second liberation. In our case it symbolized the liberation of our religious and cultural ethos, which entails praising the Creator with all languages represented and feasting on a diversity of cuisines. One of the greatest blessings was the presence of the diocesan bishop and his wife. The bishop played the guitar and also spoke about the Episcopal Church and the Anglican Communion. This made a great impression and increased the congregation's desire of being a part of the diocese.

The more we reached out to refugees and other Africans, the more we understood the diocesan vision and mission statement, particularly the phrase "community of mission outposts." We also felt compelled to obey the Great Commandment: Go therefore and make disciples of all nations, baptizing them in the name of the Father and of the Son and of the Holy Spirit, teaching them to observe all that I have commanded you; and lo, I am with you always, to the close of the age. Matthew 28:18-20. We also felt a great urge of acting out our vision statement, which is embedded in 2 Corinthians 5:18: In Christ, God was reconciling the whole world to Himself, not counting their trespasses against them. We prayed that the Spirit of God may guide us to the four colors, which is metaphor of the four corners of the earth. Within twenty months we had 135 members consisting of Black, White, Yellow, and Red. We were attracting the children of God who were bilingual or even trilingual, but were struggling to learn English.

We were also becoming more aware of the fact that God was reaching out to the Muslims through us. We invited them to Extravaganza. At first, they only entered the parish hall for food. But at our third Extravaganza they entered the church and heard the Gospel, and one of them committed his life to Christ and was baptized on Christmas. Eventually our Muslim friends participated in preparing food for Extravaganza. We joyfully discovered that Muslim ladies prepared the best-flavored dishes. Gradually the Muslims started calling me whenever they had crises and during their rites of passage. I felt honored being the priest in the community while Mary was mother of the community. They all called her Mama Mary.

The vision of the Episcopal Church in the United States was becoming clearer. A dream of increase in numbers and development of a clear vision is 20/20. In our daily prayer we ask God to help us grow in the knowledge of his will and also to grow in number. Simon repeatedly said: Our goal is to have 200 members within two years. This is in keeping with the Apostolic church in which "the Lord added to their numbers day by day those who were being saved." We have been getting new members almost every Sunday.

After worshiping in Community of Grace United Methodist Church for three months, we were surprised by St. Peter's Episcopal Church's invitation to use their facilities. Better still, St. Peter's members volunteered to assist with children ministry. Jo Snead graciously accepted the position of Sunday school director. She coordinates teachers from St. Peter's, St. Andrew's, and the University Church. Besides the use of space and the children's ministry, St. Peter's members provided our children with back to school supplies. We used their prayer books and hymnals. They provided us with office space. They prayed for us. They were indeed faithful partners in mission.

In November 2002, we were blessed by the diocese with a grant from the Loaves and Fishes Fund for $5,400. The grant was earmarked for evangelism, advertisement, vestments, altar supplies, Canterbury at Amarillo College, Christian education, and music. This grant made the members feel loved and appreciated by the diocese. Another outstanding surprise was my appointment by the bishop to minister at St. Cyprian's full-time. In Simon's words: "We are grateful for the grant, but the supreme gift that the bishop has given us is a full-time priest."

While we were enjoying a cordial relationship with godly Christians at St. Peter's, the janitor was our new Judas. Being so prejudicial to the Africans, he reported to the rector any small mess left by the children. For instance out of curiosity children would open smoking gun out of their curiosity. Instead of cleaning up (which was his duty) he would report the mess, and then I would be reprimanded by his boss. The boss was also jealous of the international congregation that was outgrowing his congregation. He also cared more about the building than he cared for the flock. Despite these challenges, our lives were characterized by celebration. Ironically, after we were kicked out of the church, the Rector was fired because of caring about the building more than the people of God.

CHAPTER TWO:
CELEBRATION FOR CIRCUMCISION

THIS DAY WAS DESIGNATED TO celebrate the circumcision of the three boys of Marko and Elizabeth. The circumcision was, however, not a rite of passage for the boys. It didn't mark their transition from childhood to adulthood. As it is the custom, the celebration starts with the host explaining why he has called the community. Marko was calling for attention and everybody was talking, and their voices were like the noise of many waters. He tried to raise his voice, but no one was listening. It was everybody trying to outshout everybody else. Children were in the bedroom, women were in the kitchen, and men were in the living room. Being the Abuna, I had to come to Marko's aid. I whistled as loudly as possible, the way I used to do when I was a shepherd boy and wanted to get the attention of the sheep, goats, or cows. To my great surprise everybody was quiet. I thought, I have pressed the right button. The women came from the kitchen with curiosity. "Who made that noise?" asked one of the ladies.

"The Abuna," responded another woman who had seen me making the noise.

"Did the Abuna make that noise? In my country that noise is made by a homeless person." It was embarrassing to note that the alarm that I had sounded was primitive and offensive.

"I was trying to get your attention," I defended myself. "What should I do if I need to get your attention?"

I now turned the offensive moment to a learning session. Seeing that no one came with an answer, I suggested, "How about if I say, 'The Lord be with you.' And then you respond, 'And also with you.'"

This pleased everybody. Since then, whenever I wanted to get their attention, I would say, "The Lord be with you." The assembly would answer, "And also with you."

After this dialogue Marko told us why we were there. He also apologized for those who didn't get the message, and that his intention was to invite everybody. He then invited us to queue for food. The Abuna must be first in the line, followed by the deacon, and then the men, women, and finally the children. In the church Mary has initiated a new method: children are first, and then they are followed by a mixture of men and women.

After the meal, Mary went to the bedroom to teach the children some gospel songs. After teaching the children, she went to the women and talked with them about home and family life.

In the meantime, I spoke with the men about spiritual things, and things related to orientating to the American way of life.

There was a great spirit of togetherness. We celebrated both individual and communal rites of passage, as well as great events of the church, such as Christmas and New Year's Day.

CHAPTER THREE:
THE FIRST CHRISTMAS

THE UNIVERSITY CHURCH HAD TAKEN our energy more than ever. We have been reviled. There had been endless complaints about my compensation. There had been an endless chorus about the closing of the church because there was no money. This of course was blamed on the priest. The prevailing feeling was that of hopelessness and doom. In all these things, we were more than conquerors in Him who loved us. This triumph is so complete that we have not only escaped unharmed, but the spirit of faithlessness and hopelessness had not destroyed our lives. The fourteen months of agony had indeed doubled our spiritual strength. We feel more equipped for the glorious ministry than ever. We can now say with St. Paul, I have fought a good fight, I have finished the race, and I have kept the Faith. Henceforth, there is laid up for me the crown of righteousness, which the Lord, the righteous judge, will award to me on that day, and not only to me but also to all that have loved his appearing.

2 Timothy 4:7-8.

Astonishingly, Mary's spirit of hospitality and generosity was enormously enhanced. She started preparing for St. Cyprian's Christmas dinner on the 22nd. She made cookies and *mandazi*. On the 24th she prepared spiral rice, coconut rice, turkey, roast beef, roast hen, and *ndengu*. She started at 8:30 p.m. and continued until 3:00 a.m.

On my part, I had to prepare the sermon. Hugh assisted me in preparing the Baptism and Eucharist Liturgy. We have to have it in a booklet form because the majority of the congregants were unfamiliar with the Book of Common Prayer. This Christmas celebration was intended to be international with African and Mexican Christian folk songs.

By 10:30 a.m. we had seventy-five people in attendance. Forty of them were little, but vibrant angels. There were so many new faces. It was my very first Christmas to have baptism. The candidate was a newly converted Muslim journalist named Sala. A few minutes before the service, Sala appeared somewhat restless. He came to me and told me he was looking for his cousin, who was to come from Dallas to attend his baptism, but he didn't know what happened to him. He asked me whether we could postpone the baptism. I told him that we were all his cousins. He finally agreed to go ahead with the baptism.

The service included carols, the Holy Baptism and the Holy Eucharist. During the Eucharist there was a surprising episode. I heard a woman shouting in a loud voice. I didn't know what she was saying, she was shouting in Dinka. As she was shouting, I saw a seven-year-old boy drop his bread. I then asked Deacon John, "What is going on?"

John responded, "She is saying, 'He is not confirmed, don't give him Holy Communion!'"

After the service we proceeded to the parish hall for the Christmas meal. Mary, Rehema, and June were in the kitchen. Everybody sat waiting to be told what to do. I was moving from one table to another to get acquainted with the new faces. There was lots of humor.

"We have utensils but no food," complained a Muslim young man. "What we need is food not utensils."

Then Mary asked me to say the blessing. Everybody was visiting with everybody else. To get their attention I shouted, "The Lord be with you!"

"And also with you," responded the congregation. Unlike in Sudanese homes, we started by serving the children, and then the adults made a queue. We then ate our dinner with gladness.

After the meal we went to Rehema's apartment. I was exhausted. I was, however, surprised at the Christmas gifts that Rehema, June, and Michele had for Mary and me. I was almost too tired to open them. After opening the gifts I went to take a nap. Before I had closed my eyes, there was a call for me from Sala. "I have something very important that I want to tell you."

"What is it?" I asked.

He said to me, "You know you are a very good man. I like your family. It is very much like my family. I am calling to say that I would like to marry your daughter, Rehema."

I was too tired to know how to react and what to say. Then I told him I would share the news with Rehema. I then lay awake in bed. I had a slight headache, which was a symptom of exhaustion, but my battery was recharged after resting. When I woke up I found Sala had already come. Rehema's body language indicated that she would have nothing to do with the new convert to Christianity. After a while Sala left. I then told Rehema about Sala's intention. She was furious.

In the evening Mary, Isaac, and I went home. We joyfully opened our gifts. It was astonishing to find that Mark, Rehema's boyfriend, and Sala had given me the same thing: cologne. I had mixed feelings about both gifts. They appeared to be political gifts. I praised God for giving me a lovely daughter, but was not sure about who was going to be my son-in-law. Mary and I were apprehensive about both of them. Nonetheless, I have always made it clear that the final decision rests with my daughter. For as the Kikuyu proverb puts it: "The ox one chooses for herself has no blemish..." And, "The meat which one chooses for himself is boneless." This was the longest Christmas Day we have ever celebrated in the United States.

I had planned to take a two-week vacation, but I was too tired to drive to Fort Hood, Texas. Besides, I wanted to clear my desk and pack the books in my office. With the hostility that leadership demonstrated, I feared that they might change the lock of my office before I got all my personal belongings. I had accumulated so many papers and books over the last six years and three months.

Even though Mary and I were exhausted, we still felt compelled by the Spirit of the Lord to reach out to the people of God.

CHAPTER FOUR:
NEW YEAR'S CELEBRATION

And they devoted themselves to the apostles' teaching and fellowship, to the breaking of bread and prayer.

ACTS 2:42

JANUARY 1, 2003, WITNESSED OUR New Year's Day celebration at Mary Kenyi's apartment. Like the early church, we have a strong spirit of togetherness. This celebration had two purposes. First, Mary offered thanksgiving to God for her flight from Sudan, moving from Dallas to Amarillo, and getting a job and an apartment. Second, we were celebrating the conversion of Sala, the first Muslim convert to the Christian faith who was baptized on Christmas Day.

The house was crowded, with men filling the living room, women in the kitchen and the first bedroom, and children in the second bedroom. We were fifty in total. We were Kenyan, Sudanese, Anglo, Native American, and Senegalese. It was noisy. Young people were watching a movie and playing computer games in the living room. I asked them to reduce the volume so that the rest of us could communicate. In the living room, there were three people in holy orders: John Mien, a deacon from Sudan; me, a Kenyan; Fr. Chris, an Anglo; Abdulai who is Senegalese and a Muslim spiritual leader; and David Bennet, a Native American.

Observing the diversity, I came up with a suggestion that we needed to name ourselves the Rainbow Christian Community. Chris and David informed us that the word rainbow has a bad history in America. It was used in the 1960s for hippie and unorthodox groups. I learned that the name had been tarnished. And so I was content with St. Cyprian's Community.

After this discussion, Deng had questions for the key people in the group. He started with Dave, who gave us a brief history of how they met and how Dave advised Deng to start a Sudanese church. Then he asked, "Dave, what is your 2003 vision for this community?"

"Now that we have a full time minister," responded Dave, "I desire that this community grow spiritually and be more committed in its Christian faith."

When it was my turn, I responded that my vision was that we increase our effort in reaching out to all the African and recent immigrants in Amarillo, and that we need to start home Bible study groups. Fr. Chris said he would like to incorporate African music in our liturgy. Josiah said he would like us to be a United African Church and we should attract all Africans in Amarillo.

I then asked Deng about his vision. He answered, "My vision is that there may be peace in Sudan.

As we were talking, I was informed that the food was ready and that I needed to say grace. As usual, everybody was visiting with everybody else. The children were noisy and women were having a good time in the kitchen talking. By this time I had learned not to whistle to get their attention. According to Dinka, this is a behavior of a homeless person. So I said with a loud voice, "The Lord is with you!"

They all responded, "And also with you." I then blessed the food.

To my dismay, Sala was gone. He came, picked up his food, and went back to his apartment. I was wondering what was happening.

Mary was organizing the kitchen. She was advising women that they didn't have to wait for men to serve themselves first. To demonstrate her point, she queued next to the clergy but the Sudanese women didn't follow her. They thought the Abuna must be first in line, followed by Father Chris, then the deacon, and then all the other men. Women then followed, while children were last. In contrast, when we have Extravaganza in the church, children are served first. Then everybody else has to line up.

After serving, Mary was with the ladies leading the discussion about important issues, such as family planning. One mother who already had six children contended, "I must have ten children. My dad told me that I must have ten children."

Mary advised, "This is America. The cost of living is very high. You need to tell your deceased father, 'Dad, this is America, and life is expensive. I cannot afford to care for ten children.'"

Following this Mary went to the children's room where there were twenty children. She taught them spiritual songs and gave them some candy. They all love "Mama Mary."

While Mary was talking to children, I was giving a homily based on John 5:24. The homily was intended to remind Sala what it means to believe in Christ: He who hears my word and believes Him who sent me, has eternal life; he does not come into judgment, but has passed from death to life. After the homily Deacon John read the same text in Arabic and gave a summary of the message.

Subsequently, we decided to visit Sala. Six men and my wife went with me. We found him with the older son of Mary Kenyi and asked why he didn't stay at the party. He told us how he was missing his family. Men seemed to know his ultimate concern: To marry the priest's daughter. To my dismay, my friends seemed not only to give him false assurance, but also pressured him to marry as soon as possible. One of them suggested that he should marry within sixty days. They all had an eye on my first-born daughter. We were now experiencing a conflict between Sudanese and Kenyan cultures. In Sudan, a father may decide who will marry his daughter; in Kenya, male and female may fall in love, and then the young man has to request permission from the parents of the girl. Prior to this time, I had informed Sala about our custom, but he was unconvinced. After advising my brethren not to rush Sala into marriage, Mary and I decided to leave. Sala escorted us to our car. It was very cold, but Sala told us that he liked cold weather.

Mary and I observed that Sala represented a different culture and social class. He was from Northern Sudan and spoke only Arabic. He is an Arab. His grandfather was a minster of transportation, and his Dad inherited the same ministry. His brothers and sisters lived in different Europeans countries and had international marriages. He did not fit in well in Dinka culture, and felt that he fit in my family much better. He saw us as upper class and this was why he persistently asked me to give him my daughter in marriage.

CHAPTER FIVE:
PASTORAL VISITS
REACHING OUT TO THE MUSLIM FAMILIES

ON JANUARY 11, 2003, THE Spirit led us to the Muslim families. We started with Ibrahim's family. They have attended Extravaganza several times. We have also attended a party in their home. They own a middle class home and have three vehicles.

We were warmly welcomed. Ibrahim was not home, but the mother and her three children were there. It was very noisy as the TV's volume was high . A four-year-old boy had earphones from a CD player plugged in his ears. He was hyper and aggressive. He held two remote controls. With one he controlled his TV and with the other the TV in the living room. Takwa, the twelve-year-old, first-born daughter sat with me and showed me a family album, while Mary was talking with the mother. I asked Takwa to lower the volume of the TV and she obeyed. Mary had carried candies for the children, but before she gave the candies, the mother gave us candies and soda. But we both opted to drink water.

From the family photo we learned that the family is of three worlds. Sudan is their first world and Lebanon is their second. They resided in Lebanon for five years before proceeding to the United States. At home they speak Arabic. While Ibrahim speaks in the vernacular, Hayawed speaks Arabic and "a little English." Her two daughters are fluent in English and Arabic. Ahmad speaks a mixture of English and Arabic. He doesn't express himself well in any of these languages and this makes him very aggressive. We also observed that Ibrahim was a Sudanese policeman while Hayawed was an actor.

Every member of the family has high self-esteem. Takwa wants to become a medical doctor while her sister Fatima wants to be an actor. The mother hopes for a four-bedroom house so that each child may have her/his own bedroom. She thinks this would reduce sibling fighting.

After staying for 45 minutes, we stood and told them that we needed to go. Hayawed told us that she had called Ibrahim and that we have to wait for him. After waiting for 15 minutes we bid them farewell. We headed to the Surrs.

As we were pulling into the parking lot of the apartment, we saw Fred and Fatuma driving behind us and we waited for them. Fred is a Congolese and Fatuma is Senegalese. They were speaking in French. No sooner had they alighted than we greeted them. I spoke with Fred while Mary talked with Fatuma. I was conversing in Swahili. Turning to Fatuma, I spoke to her in the same language, not realizing that she doesn't speak in Swahili. She looked apprehensive. For a while I didn't understand why she was not responding. Then it dawned on me that I was using a language that was as Greek to Fatuma. I then apologized and I talked to her in English. She invited us to her apartment. Fred bid us farewell.

Entering the house we found everything was scattered in the living room. She apologized and told us that she has a two-and-half-year-old who jumps everywhere and scatters everything around. We told her that we had a boy who did the same thing. Coumba, who is ten, helped her mom clear the room. As soon as we sat, Fatuma brought us large glasses of orange juice. It seems that Africans have one common heritage: generosity. They are the most generous creatures that God has made.

As we were talking, Abdualaye came in wearing traditional African attire. We expressed great admiration for the outfit. Fatuma then told us that she had made it. She then brought some clothes that she had made. She said she wished to move to a place where there are more Africans who would buy her clothes.

Mary, who has a great gift for details, started asking them about the family. They told us that they have six children. Their daughter and son are working at IBP and reside in their own apartment.

"But they are very lazy," complains the Father. "They work at night for eight hours and they sleep the whole day while I work overtime and go to school full-time. Most of the time I have only two hours of sleep."

"It takes a village to rear a child," I commented.

This was where we needed to step in. Mary praised their daughter. "She is so beautiful. She can be a model." After a long conversation we asked them whether they would like to join us for regular worship in the church. They told us that they attend mosque and that they are expected to pray five times a day. But they were sorry to miss our Christmas celebration. They were given wrong directions and for that reason they could not find the church. Now they know where the church is and will be attending Extravaganza.

In the course of our conversation we learned that Abdulaye is a Tunisian while Fatuma is a Senegalese. In Tunisia the Africans have suffered at the hand of the Arabs.

The challenge facing this family is that Fatuma has type 1 diabetes. She takes two insulin shots every day and is pregnant. Because of this, she is not working but has a small income for her disability. Yet the family is confident that things will be better.

After visiting with them for fifty minutes we told them we had to go. They persuaded us to stay a bit longer. We insisted that we had to go. Even though it was very cold, Abdulaye escorted us to our car. We felt a bond with this family. We praised God for connecting us to this family.

Two months after this visit, Mohamed, the fifteen-year-old son of Abdulaye, came to church with David, Mary Kenyi's son. He came for healing. He had a constant headache. So I asked him to come forward to the altar. Kneeling down I prayed for him and he was healed. He became connected to the church.

On March 7, 2003, I visited Muslim families. This time Mary was too tired to visit with me. I started with the Abdulaye family. Coumba opened the door and then hid behind the door. Fatuma was lying on the couch very pregnant. She was delighted to see me. After the greetings she asked, "Where is your wife?"

"She has been very busy today and was too tired to come with me," I responded. "How have you been?"

"I am tired," she responded. "My doctor told me that I should be having the baby in three weeks. I have lost my appetite because I have to have two insulin shots every day for diabetes. I also check my blood sugar twice."

As we were talking, three-year-old Ibrahim started climbing the chair. I asked him to come and give me a hug. After a hug he wanted to play ball with me. Then I asked Coumba about her school. She told me that she loves all her teachers. She also likes all the subjects. Her Mom informed me that Coumba, Ayak, and Nono were interviewed on TV yesterday. I was very proud of the family. After twenty minutes I asked them to pray with me. We held our hands together and prayed. I felt a great peace emanating from the Unitive Being. After this I headed to Sadiq's family.

After knocking at the door, Hayawed came to answer the door. She was delighted to see me. "Where's Mary?" she queried. I told her that Mary had a long day and for that reason she was unable to come with me. "Everybody is busy," she generalized. She then gave me a seat. She was watching a story on the Arabic channel. I told her how I would like to speak Arabic and that if it were not for the alphabet, I would learn it easily because Swahili has some commonality with Arabic. She said, "Yes, some similar words include salamu and shetani." After visiting with her I informed her about the forthcoming Gospel Extravaganza, and then we parted. I now headed to the Mexican family of Jorge & Maria Teresa Gonzales.

A VISIT TO THE MEXAN FAMILY

THIS IS THE FIRST VISIT to this family. I knocked on the door but nobody answered. I went to the backyard and saw Maria leashing a dog. When she saw me she welcomed me in the house. The house was well kept. There were flowers on the coffee table with six candles. I commended her for the neatness of her house. She then showed me their wedding photo and the family picture. She has nine sisters and five brothers. Her father is seventy-two and the mother is sixty-five. While she was showing me the pictures Jorge came from the bedroom. After a greeting he said, "Father, we have been waiting for you since 3:00 p.m."

"But I told you that I was coming at 5:00 p.m. I am sorry for keeping you waiting," I apologized.

"It is okay, Father," he spoke forgivingly. He then gave me his family photo, which included him, Rocio, and his younger sister. He told me that they are the only three in the family. Unlike Maria, he didn't talk about his father and mother.

"How many children are you planning to have?"

"No more than three," Maria answered emphatically.

"But you are fourteen in your family,' I commented jokingly.

"But none of my brothers or sisters has more than three."

"Tell me about your wedding."

Jorge told me that they were married seven years ago and he does not remember the name of the priest who solemnized their marriage. But they married in a Roman Catholic Church since Maria is a Catholic.

"But I like your church," responded Maria. "We would like to be members."

I then led them in a discussion about the similarities and differences between the two traditions. A similarity included the holy orders: bishop, priest, and deacon, and the liturgy. I then talked more about the strength of the Anglican Church, that it rested on three pillars: tradition, scripture, and reason. I then asked them whether they had a Bible. Maria brought two Bibles to me. One was the Revised Standard Version, the other was a Spanish Bible. Both had pictures and appeared to be children's Bibles. George asked me whether I would get them a Spanish Bible. I told him that I would try to get them one.

I then talked about St. Cyprian's and the Sunday school program, which uses the Catechesis of the Good Shepherd. Jorge interrupted proudly and said, "I don't need someone to teach my children catechism. I can do that myself."

I then explained to him about the program and told him that it takes a village to rear a child. "You cannot do it alone."

Maria then brought up the subject about her children receiving communion. "When we are taking communion, we are taking the body and the blood of Jesus." She said this in Spanish while her husband was interpreting. "A child cannot understand this. I wouldn't like my children to take communion until they are nine." I then told her that was okay.

After that Jorge told me that he would like to do something in the church but is limited because he doesn't speak English well. I subsequently told him that most of our members are learning English and that when he becomes a member, I will give him something to do.

After that he told me that he values his children so much that his wife has to stay at home and take care of them. "I always tell my sister that you cannot depend on the day care to take care of your children." I commended him for this but I didn't want to comment about Rocio who is a black sheep in the family.

After the fruitful visit, I bid them farewell. As I pulled away, I was hearing two voices. One was a high voice, the other a low voice. The high voice told me that I needed to visit Rocio as well. The low voice told me that I have done enough for the day and that I was tired. But I opted to listen to the higher voice.

Knocking at the door I was warmly received by the children. It seems that I am the most cherished member of the family. Zeus, a four-year-old son, started playing with his fingers, as I played with mine. Rocio asked me whether I would like to drink something, coffee, apple juice, or water. I preferred apple juice. Zeus, one of the most handsome boys under the sun, looked at me lovingly while holding an orange. "Would like an orange?"

"No, thank you." The love and hospitality that I am accorded is replenishing my body and spirit. Rocio looked depressed. She pulled over the chair and sat near the sink.

She was ready to tell me about the fight she had with Carlos, a fight that resulted in the cancellation of the blessing of their marriage. "Father," she started narrating the incident, "I was talking about my nephew. I said that he is beautiful. Then Carlos got angry with me and spit on me. I then hit him with a frying pan. After the fight he left and didn't come back till six in the morning."

"Have you ever stayed for a month without a fight?" I queried.

"No."

"Is he still with you?"

"Yes, but we don't talk to each other. When he is in the house I go to the back yard. When he comes to the backyard, I come to the house.

I am not going to live with him. He works twelve hours a day for seven days and then lies to me that he gets only $100. He is supposed to pay the water bill, but has not done so and I am afraid that the city is going to cut off the water. I have so many unpaid bills, and Carlos says that he cannot pay them because they are in my name. The reason is because he doesn't have legal documents. [This means that he is an illegal immigrant.] I am tired of him giving excuses that he cannot pay the bills because they are in my name. I am tired and angry with him for spitting on my children and me." The tears were rolling on her cheeks.

I am also perturbed for the lack of any easy answer. I told her that they both have to learn to live together. After listening to her and giving her words of encouragement, I call the whole family for prayer. We held hands together. As I was praying, Zeus repeated after me while Rocio was sobbing with tears. After the prayer, Mitsy looked straight in her mother's eye and said, "Don't cry, mom. I love you." She then kissed her mother lovingly and hugged her. I indeed saw the face of Jesus on the face of this child. I then bid them farewell and drove home. I arrived home at 7:30 p.m.

PASTORAL VISIT TO THE DYING

March 19, 2003, is cold, wet, and windy. Mary and I were paying pastoral visits. The previous night Mary was on duty at the Palo Duro Retirement Village, where she worked from 2:00 a.m. to 8:00 a.m. She returned home at 8:15 a.m., went to bed at 9:00 a.m. and slept until noon. I was astonished at her willingness to accompany me for pastoral visits. What dedication! Being on a hospice pastoral team, she had to make a pastoral visit to Sarah (this is not her real name), an Indian woman whose deceased husband was a medical doctor. This productive and ailing mother has five children, all of whom were doctors. This Christian lady had lived in Tanzania, and for that reason she speaks Swahili. Mary is the only person on the hospice team who speaks Swahili.

It was raining when we pulled into her driveway. Mary left me in the car and went to minister to her. After twenty minutes she came back more peaceful and joyous. They had prayed together and recited the verse that Sarah had learned as a child: "For God so loved the world that He gave his only son, that whosoever believed in him should not perish but have eternal life." John 3:16. They also sang:

Jesus love of my soul;
Let me to Thy bosom fly.

After this we drove to Fatuma's place. On the way Mary insisted that we go to the store to buy presents for the newly born. We drove to the Dollar General only to discover that neither of us had money and the store didn't take credit cards. Mary remembered that she had her checkbook in her purse. I rushed for it when it started raining on me. We bought the presents and drove to the Surr's home. Fatuma was jubilant when she saw us. She said: "I called your home several times on Monday but there was no response! I wanted to tell you the good news. That after you came here last Friday and prayed for me. I told him that I was expecting to deliver in three weeks, but the baby came three days after your visit. I had a safe delivery."

We told her that the telephone might have been off the hook. A few minutes later Abulaye came. We asked Fatuma to bring the baby. Holding a handsome 8.5 pound baby boy fueled our joy. His name is Ahemand. "He had lot of hair, but we cut it," Fatuma said. "According to our custom, we believe that birth hair is a bad omen." Then we discussed the naming system. According to Muslims, boys are named after the prophets. That is why we have many men who are named Musa, Ibrahim, and Mohamed, etc. Before we departed Fatuma asked us to pray. After calling all in the house, we held our hands together in a circle and prayed. She now strongly believes in the power of prayer.

We also invited them to our Extravaganza, which will be in three weeks.

It was still raining as we were going to the car to drive to the Gonzales', our Mexican new members. It was a twenty-minute drive. I had called Maria Teresa, who told me that her husband was sick. So I told her that I would try to visit with them today. It was still raining when we pulled into their driveway. After knocking at the door, we waited for a while. There was no response. Mary advised me to be patient. After a few minutes I knocked again. There was no sound. I knocked a third time. There was no response. The incident reminded me of two precious verses: "I slept, but my heart was awake. Hark! My beloved is knocking. Open to me, my sister, my love, my dove, my perfect one, for my head is wet with dew." Song of Solomon 5:2. And, "Behold, I stand at the door and knock, if any one hears my voice and opens the door, I will come in to him and eat with him he with me." Revelation 3:20.

After this we wanted to visit Mary Kenyi, a Sudanese single mother, and Father Chris, a celibate priest who ministers with me, but the rain was pouring down heavily. So we decided to visit our daughters. After being refreshed with a cup of tea we drove home.

Surprisingly, we were not hungry, even though it was past 6:00 p.m. and we went without lunch. We remembered our Master's Word: "My food," said Jesus, "is to do the will of him who sent me and to finish his work." John 4:34.

CHAPTER SIX:
BIBLE STUDY

During the New Year's celebration we resolved that we were going to start Bible study. Just as the church was born in a home, we were fully convinced that it be sustained by home fellowship.

Mary Kenyi, who hosted the New Year's celebration, was generous enough to host the group. The first session was held on January 14, 2003. We had ten people in attendance. To my great surprise, Mary had several Bibles in different versions, which were enough for those who didn't have Bibles.

The Spirit led me to do it differently. I spent more time giving background of the text and doing hermeneutics. I then asked each person to share the phrase and verse that he/she liked most. To my surprise, the first comment was, "Before we get to that I have a question." The questions were very engaging with an overtone of mutual challenge. Here are some of the questions: "Can I say that I love God while I hate Mary?"

Mary interjected, "Don't hate me!"

This led us to what the Bible says about brotherly love. "If one says I love God and hates his brother, he is a liar, for he who does not love his brother whom he has seen, cannot love God whom he has not seen." Eventually, I discovered that teaching, listening, and asking questions was the method that the groups enjoyed.

ROTATING FROM ONE HOME TO ANOTHER

After meeting in Mary's place for several weeks, the numbers attending started declining. One day after the Bible study, Beny, the bishop's brother, saw me privately.

"I am suggesting that we rotate from one home to another. Do not ask them for their opinion. Just tell them that from now on we will be holding our study in different homes. But don't tell anybody that I suggested this to you."

"Thank you, "I responded. "I will keep this to myself."

The following Saturday I did as Beny had suggested. We agreed that we would meet in the Garang home for the whole month of March. I had already discussed with the Garangs and so the decision pleased both the fellowship and the Garang family.

Taking a Bible study to this home was a healing process for both Maikil and Angelina. Angelina was the lady who shouted on Christmas during communion, commanding us not to give her son the Eucharist. After this Mary and I made several visits. We learned that what she was saying was that her son was not baptized and so he should not receive Holy Communion. So in February we baptized their three children. They also had another disappointment. When they bought their new home, they spent $700 for a housewarming party. But to their great disappointment nobody came. Now that the whole church is gathering in their home, they are joyous. Even though I discouraged the hosts from providing refreshments, Angelina felt compelled to serve tea and donuts. She reminds me of the St. George's men's Bible study at which Glen and Bill provided donuts.

On the first day there were fourteen people. The living room was well kept and furnished. Angelina is very artistic. We had Bibles in English,

Arabic, and French. But we mostly discussed in English. Occasionally, the Dinka would speak in Dinka, and Regina, Simon's wife, would shout, "English please!" This does not bother us because, like Dinka (the largest ethnic group is Sudan), I was used to it when I was in Kenya. As usual, the discussion is interesting. A twenty-one-year-old Congolese posed a question, "Should we follow you or what the Bible says?"

Angelina interjected authoritatively, "We must follow the priest, for he knows the word of God better. But when he deviates from the scriptures we should follow the scriptures." After the Bible study Maikil and Angelina provided us with soda and water.

On March 15, I had another surprise. We had seven people attending and opened the study with prayer. Then everyone opened his Bible. I noticed that Angelina didn't have a Bible. I said that we had planned to have a Bible for everyone. Looking at me with a smile and a twinkle in her eyes, Angelina said, "I never learned how to read in any language." That's how we discovered she was illiterate. I was so proud of her for the way she waited for us with readiness. And the manner in which she theologically reflected on the text. I learned that to be an angel one does not need to be literate.

We prayed for Angelina's mother and brother who were still waiting for papers to be processed. We prayed also for Fatuma, who delivered yesterday. Even though she is Muslim, she is a part of our fellowship.

The key questions for us today was, Do you want to be healed? What do you want God to do for you?

What is the specific prayer request for our church? We prayed that God would help our members be more regular, punctual, and committed.

CHAPTER SEVEN:
THE LIGHT TO THE NATIONS

THIS MORNING I MEET WITH junior and senior high school youth. As usual I called them the day before to remind them. I called Abuk and her answer was, "I will not be able to come because my dad and mom are working this Saturday." She is indeed an assistant parent. I then called Sarah who told me that she is coming with her sister Lois. I called Peter who agreed that he would be there together with his brother David.

I was driving from Canyon to Amarillo. After driving for ten minutes I remembered that I had forgotten the church key. I decided to go by faith. I picked up Sarah and her sister. I was at Peter's and decided that we would hold our Bible study at Peter's home. There was a young man who had slept overnight at Peter's so he joined the group. No sooner had we started when three other young men flocked in. I now had Sudanese, Congolese, and African Americans in attendance. We read John 9. Sarah had more to say during the discussion than any other person. There are several key words in these verses: "Neither this man nor his parents sinned, but the work of God should be revealed in him." We are learning that we are all precious. We were born that way to glorify God.

The other key verse is: "Go, wash in the pool of Siloam [which translated as sent]." We are learning that we must participate in our own healing.

We were also enlightened by Jesus' claim: "As long as I am in the world, I am the light of the world." We were learning that Jesus is our guide in the dark world. He is indeed the way, the truth, and the life.

We were now halfway through the discussion. I suggested that we order a pizza. One of the boys who had flocked in said that his mom had a coupon. We asked him to go and get it. Three of them left. They delayed coming back. I would be late for the adult Bible study. They came and ordered pizza. Sarah and Lois refused to eat pizza. I asked them why they were not eating. Lois whispered to me, "We cannot eat in front of them." I felt sorry for them. I was now 15 minutes late for the next Bible study. So I grabbed a piece of pizza and ate hurriedly, and then I left with Sarah and Lois. After dropping them at their place I headed to Mabure's. I found Deacon John standing outside, chatting with two men. He said, "Pastor John, five men were here for Bible study and they have left." I apologized for keeping Sudanese time.

Sadiq corrected me. "It is not Sudanese time, it is African time."

It was getting too hot to stay outside so Deacon John asked us to go in the house. It was now Sadiq, a Muslim, and Mengar. The discussion was about rearing children and about how to spend our money wisely. It was a fruitful discussion. Amir refreshed us with a cup of tea. After this I headed home. As I drove, I was praising God for allowing me to forget the key to the church. He knew very well that he had a key to the new boys and to my Muslim friends. He is indeed the light of the world.

CHAPTER EIGHT:
JESUS GREW

JUNIOR ACOLYTES

Jesus grew both in body and wisdom, gaining favor with God and man.
LUKE 2:52

THIS MORNING WE WERE DRIVING with Benson, a nephew who is staying with me for the summer holiday. He assisted me in everything. He is to me as John Mark was to Paul. We headed to Libscomb to transport the junior acolytes, who are seven and twelve years old. As we approached Simon's home, Santo, a compulsive six year old boy, is the first to come to the car. He is very ready to go. "Pastor John, I am going with you. I want to be an acolyte."

"Not this time, I came for your sisters," I responded.

The little boy ran back to the house, crying with a loud voice. I felt sorry for him. Agor and Rheta were coming while Abuk was consoling her brother. We drove to the Kimfilas to pick up Nono who was ready. We drove on to St. Peter's. This time there was no activity in the parish hall. So we sat in a circle and enjoyed the doughnuts and soda.

Luke 2:41-52 was our passage for discussion. Each acolyte had to read a few verses. Then Benson had to read the story again. We are using the method of asking and answering questions. To my complete surprise, these children are very much like the boy Jesus. They were asking profound theological questions. "Was Joseph a father of Jesus?" asked Rheta.

"The answer is yes and no," I responded. "He was his father in the sense that he reared Jesus as an adoptive father. But God was actually his Father because Mary became pregnant through the power of the Holy Spirit. This is why Jesus asked his parents, 'Why do you have to look for me? Didn't you know that I have to be in my Father's house?'"

"My sister told me that God put a piece of himself in Mary's stomach so that he may save us," Rheta added.

"That is another way of putting it. Let us put it this way, 'In Jesus, God became what we are so as to make us what he is.' In the Gospel according to John we read, 'The Word (who was God) became a human being, full of grace and truth, and lived among us. We saw his glory, the glory that he received as the Father's only Son'". John 1:14.

Now Agor's hand went up. "Pastor John, let's go and do acolyte practice!"

"We have to do the memory verse first."

We start to memorize Luke 2:52: "Jesus grew both in body and wisdom, gaining favor with God and man." After the memory verse we headed to the church. That morning we concentrated on processing, recessing, and manners. They all seemed to enjoy it.

After practice we drove back home, singing with lot of wit:

> *Read your Bible,*
> *Pray every day,*
> *If you want to grow.*

CHAPTER NINE:
DO NOT BE AFRAID

Mary and I drove the Honda Civic 2000 that morning. We stopped at a donut shop to buy a dozen doughnuts. As we neared I-27, I remembered that we had more children than we could accommodate in our car. Maikil had volunteered to assist with transportation, but he was working this morning. Rocio had promised me that she would bring five Spanish children. But whether she fulfills her promise depends on whether there was a fight between her and her husband. May car would only take five children and for that reason, some children were to be left. So I knocked at Simon's door. Abuk answered the door. "We are just waking up. Go and pick up Nono first and then come for us."

"No! I will wait for them."

"I do not have their breakfast ready."

"Tell them to prepare themselves as soon as possible."

At the meantime Santo came with his request. "Pastor John, I want to go with you."

"No. I am taking your sisters." His tears were running down his cheeks. I was moved with compassion. "Go and prepare yourself." Within four minutes the children were ready to go. Santo was first in the car. Mary discovered that Santo did not wash his face. She asked Rheta to bring a wet towel. Rheta wiped his brother's face. We drove to Nono's and he was ready. At St. Peter's, Rosio and her five children were nowhere to be found.

We met at the parish hall. After prayer we ate doughnuts. Mary asked for this opportunity to teach them manners. "You don't talk with food in your mouth. You don't put both your elbows on the table, etc." After the dos and don'ts we asked them to add to their list. "Do not be kidnapped!"

"What do you do to avoid being kidnapped?" I posed this question for discussion. The list included do not ride with a stranger, do not talk to a stranger, do not walk alone. Stay close to your parents.

"What would you do if you are being kidnapped?" The list included kick, fight, scream.

"Let someone scream for me the way you would scream if you are being kidnapped." Agor's hand went up. She screamed with a loud voice.

This was followed with singing "Read your Bible, pray every day." We studied Mark 6:45-52. We started with a memory verse: "Jesus spoke to them at once, 'Courage!' he said. 'It is I, don't be afraid!'" Then playing the role of Andrew I told them how we spent the day with Jesus, and how I saw him walking on the water and how he came to the boat. After this the children read the story. I was astonished to note that Santo, who is in kindergarten, can read. He was right when he insisted that he must come with us.

CHAPTER TEN:
SPEAK LORD

Speak Lord, your servant is listening.
I Samuel 3:9

At times African youth can be nasty to each other, while they are tender to American youth. So I started the discussion with the question, "Why should we as Africans be nice to each other?" The answer was: Because we all came from the same continent. We need to give each other moral support. And because we are Christians and Jesus has told us to love one another.

The second question was, "What challenges do you face as African youth?"

"They say that we don't know how to speak English. We are asked embarrassing questions such as, Do you have running water in Africa? Do you eat gum from the tree? Did you wear any clothes before you came to the United States?"

Sarah, a Congolese, told us how his dad deals with the question about clothes. He simply tells them that we don't wear clothes in Africa. Another young man was asked how he came to America. "Did you come by bus?"

"No!" he responded. "I swam."

"How long did it take you to swim to America?"

"Three weeks."

"Three weeks!" exclaimed the surprised friend.

"You must be a good swimmer."

After this discussion we read the call of Samuel, 1 Samuel 3. We learned that Samuel started like an acolyte and was assisting Eli at the sanctuary. We learned that the ministry of the acolyte goes way back to the Old Testament. We learned that God appeared to this boy at a particular period. There were few messages or visions from the Lord in those days. The Lord also called Samuel at a particular time and place. He was called from the sanctuary where the sacred covenant box was kept. God called to him at night, but the boy thought it was Eli calling. And so he went to Eli and responded, "Here am I." We learned that the call is not always clear in the beginning. Yet God will continue calling until we become fully aware He is calling us.

When we accept the call, we become connected to the power source. It is vital that we stay connected otherwise we remain powerless. If we unplug, we are as useless as an electronic device that is disconnected.

We learned that when the Lord calls us, he gives us a particular ministry. Samuel became a priest, prophet and judge. The calling process started long before Samuel was born. It started with his mother's intense prayer at the altar. She prayed, "Lord Almighty, look at me your servant! See my trouble and remember me! Do not forget me! If you give me a son, I promise that I will dedicate him to you for his whole life and that he will never have his hair cut."

We learned that there are some people who pray for us. But it is important that we listen to the Lord. We also learned the importance of the ministry at the altar. Because God called the great prophets like Samuel and Isaiah from the sanctuary.

As usual we are looking for a phrase, a clause, or a sentence that touches our heart. The words that stand out this morning are "Speak, Lord, your servant is listening."

CHAPTER ELEVEN:
I CAN DO ALL THINGS THROUGH CHRIST

I can do all things through Him who strengthens me.
PHILIPPIANS 4:13

JUNE 7 2003

I HAD PLANNED TO TAKE Isaac to a basketball tournament, visit the Temple of Praise church, have lunch with the Gonzales family, and visit with Simeon Aloak.

At 10:00 a.m. I dropped Isaac at Palo Duro High School. He wanted me to watch the game with him, but I felt that this was the only Saturday I had for visiting the Temple of Praise. I had, however, to search for it as though I was searching for a particle of gold in the sand. After 45 minutes I located a small church at 209 N. Adams. The church is located in the Black neighborhood. I felt bad for being so late because this church family attended our Extravaganza.

To my surprise, when I opened the door, there were only three people in the pews, one of them being a bishop. At the podium was a preacher who was well dressed. He was using *Standard Lesson Commentary: International Sunday School Lesson* by Standard Publishing. I was warmly welcomed.

A copy of the study book was handed to me. The preacher employed dialogic methods similar to what we use in our Bible study. The bishop who was sitting in the pew did as much teaching as the preacher.

At 11:20 a.m. the people of God flocked in. They included women and youth. I learned that these friends have the same concept of time as my folks. The latecomers fully participated in the dialogue.

The bishop was speaking strongly against having women in leadership in church. They must be under the leadership of a man. As soon as he finished speaking, a lady raised her hand and asked, "What if the man neglects his job?" She then answered herself. "I believe in this regard woman must take leadership."

"If the man cannot lead," insisted the bishop, "his wife can assist but should not take the leadership. The man must be the head of the household."

Having ministered to African Americans for twelve years, I found the bishop very courageous since 60% of black families are headed by mothers. The bishop had a good knowledge of Pauline literature, but was lacking in the knowledge of human reality.

Being a guest I didn't want to say much, but I was asked to say something. I then expressed my gratitude for their participation in our Extravaganza and I invited them to the banquet.

At noon, I asked for permission to leave since I had a Bible study at noon. At 12:15 p.m. I was at the Mabure residence where we had Bible study. We discussed the Fourth Gospel. We had to read the Bible both in English and Arabic. Deacon John had to interpret in Dinka because we had a family that had just come from Sudan who had not yet learned any English.

Interestingly, when women became the subject, the issue was totally different. My Dinka friends were talking about bride price. In one clan the dowry is one hundred head of cattle, while in another it is thirty head of cattle. In some clans where women are lazy, you can get one for free. If you marry from a chief's family, you will be given more animals. Interestingly, nobody seemed to be offended by the discussion. And no one saw a contradiction between the African custom and Biblical teaching. It also goes without saying that Dinka women have very high self-esteem and are proud they are so valued.

At 1:45 p.m. I realized that I was late for our lunch with Rocio and Carlos and their children. So I told my friends that I had to leave. I called Rocio with my cell phone and told her that I was running late. "Okay, Father," she responded graciously, "we will wait for you."

I was late two minutes. When Zeus their five-year-old son saw me he ran to me and jumped on my shoulders. Omer and Mitsy came and embraced me affectionately. The passersby were surprised to see a black priest engulfed by yellow beautiful children. Rocio led us to the food where we had all you can eat.

"We were here eight months ago," commented Carlos. I recalled how I had to wait for them for one hour. That time they were my guests. This time they were reciprocating.

For eight months they had gone through so much. Twice we had planned to bless their marriage. But in two incidents they had to cancel the marriage ceremony because of a physical fight. Rocio had asked Carlos to leave. He left and came back. He stood in the church and confessed that he had been drinking beer and taking drugs and had decided to quit. He concluded his confession with, "I love my family." I had to give him some counseling and recommended him to Alcoholics Anonymous. He has now been sober and has a job. Things seemed much better.

As we were halfway through our lunch some issues surfaced that called for family counseling. Rocio complained that Carlos does not listen to her when she is pouring out her problems. "It is always the same things," responded Carlos.

"You still need to listen to her and let her cry on your shoulders," I advised.

"Cry over my shoulders all the day long?" he exaggerated.

Remember the shortest verse in the Bible. "Jesus wept."

"I pour my problems out to you because I know you are strong." She now said something positive about him for the first time. She also complained that Carlos didn't share with her what was bothering him.

"Instead of sharing with her I go the park," he said, justifing himself.

We then discussed the importance of sharing and that men share their feelings in different ways. Rocio also complained that her daughter spends more time with her friends than she spends with her. We talked about forgiveness and gratitude. The whole session took two and a half hours. We then hugged and bid each other farewell. I drove to Simon's for my last appointment.

As I drove to Simon's residence, I was moved with deep feeling to the point of shedding tears. I was thanking God for finding me worthy to share the struggle of this Mexican family. I thanked God for their openness and the gradual healing that was taking place. I was also weeping because I knew that my ministry with them was ending soon. They are indeed in need of a physician. They had made use of my counseling and conflict management skills more than any other family. I loved them as the shepherd loves his lambs. They are indeed priceless and it was indeed worthwhile to suffer with and for them.

A FIRE FIGHTER

I knocked at the door and Agor answered. She made her regular and consistent request. "Pastor John, am I going to be an alcolater? [She meant acolyte.] "I am already seven and I will soon be eight. Please! Please! Please! I can do it. This is how you walk as an acolater." She then walked with her hands together like a saint. I sat down and every child wanted to sit with me. Rheta and Abuk were in the kitchen. I was somewhat exhausted but still having fun with the kids. As we enjoyed ourselves I saw smoke in the kitchen. All the children ran out. I dashed to the kitchen and discovered a fire in the trash can. I filled a bucket with water and put out the fire. Where did the fire come from?

Rheta toasted bread on the stove burner and it caught fire. She threw it into the garbage can when it was still burning. I understood that God planned for me to be there to fight the fire. Both parents were working. Abuk, thirteen, was the one who was taking care of the children.

Simon was nowhere to be found for our appointment. I headed home, spent out. I am going straight to bed for a nap. I woke at 10:00 p.m., confused about the day. I didn't know whether it was Friday or Saturday or Sunday. I remembered a scripture, "They that trust the Lord will renew their strength."

While the Lord was renewing my strength, I was agonizing the fact that the ecclesiastical authority perceived the ministry to all nations as a deviation from the "job for which I was hired." I was hired to minister to affluent European Americans, not blue-collar workers who were African and Mexican. And for this extracurricular activity plans were underway to phase me out. The financial support from the diocese was coming to an end.

CHAPTER TWELVE:
BAD TIDINGS AND RECONCILIATIONS

When I reported to St. Cyprian's church committee that the bishop had resolved to discontinue financial support, to my utter surprise the members showed no sign of faithlessness and hopelessness. The spirit of meanness, scarcity, and doom that I wrestled with in my previous cure is not in these people who have so little. The first comment from Simon was "It is God's mission. God will support it."

After a long discussion the committee resolved that:

We will hold a fundraising banquet.

The bishop's committee will visit the bishop and give their side of the story.

The banquet will be held on July 6, 2003. They will invite their friends and each working adult member of the church will contribute $25. Angelina, who hosted the committee members and who is full of humor commented, "We should not only give during this special occasion, we must give every Sunday. When the plate was being passed on Sunday, I closed one eye and looked through the corner of the other eye, only to see some people dropping 25 cents in the plate. We should not give God 25 cents."

One of the biggest challenges of refugee Christians is to move from being recipients to givers. They come to church to receive. And when they give, they give either pennies or a dollar. As Angelina was suggesting, they needed to know that there are more blessings in giving than in receiving, and that God loves a cheerful giver.

CHAPTER THIRTEEN: HERE IT COMES AGAIN

THE QUESTION "WHY ME?" IS coming again. It is invading my study room. It is interfering with my meditation. It is coming with a spirit of hopelessness. This was the prevailing demon, the demon that took the University Church to captivity during my last year of ministry. It regarded the word faith as naiveté. The steward of abundance was replaced with the steward of scarcity and meanness. I now smell the same spirit.

I was still glued to the vicarage. My study room was closest to the church building, the place where endless meetings and plottings were held. I indeed smelled an offensive odor. The smell which is worse than that of cow dung from the feedlot. This was the spirit whose intention was to rob me of the four great virtues: faith, love, joy, and peace.

I was trying to put things into perspective. I now understood that even though I have been in the United States for twenty-one years, I am still perceived by the ecclesiastical leadership as a representative of the Global South. Unknowingly, I have established a church of the blackest people on the African continent. The church that has a big dread of converting the Muslims, that have persecuted them, that killed their fathers, mothers, brothers, and sisters, and has taken their loved ones to slavery. This is the church at the cutting edge. The church that was valueless to ecclesiastical authority. At the grassroots we perceive the golden opportunity of competing with Islamization and secularism.

Yet the leadership does not want to spend financial resources with this ministry. I was one of three missioners in the diocese. In addition to me, one ministers to the white congregation and the other to Hispanics. The three of us were diocesan employees. I am the only one with black skin. The "latest to be hired and first to be fired."

I tried to study to put my little world in perspective of the global village. I was reading an article in the *Anglican Digest*, "Global South Christendom: Is it Inevitable?" by Prof. Stephen Noll. Father Noll makes enlightened observations. He rightly contends that "Christianity may be winning the numbers game in the Global South against Islam and secularism, but it is not consolidating these gains at the leadership level." He observes that in Uganda the Muslims are outspending the Christians many times over in higher education. He writes, "The organization of Islamic States recently opened 'King Faud Plaza' in downtown Kampala, a $10 million high rise which houses the downtown campus of the Islamic University. By contrast, the Anglican Church has been attempting without success to raise even $1 million for a Church House to help fund pensions for the clergy, who presently retire penniless." Deacon John Mien, a Sudanese who ministers with me, has told me repeatedly how they could not compete with Muslims in Sudan because Muslims use two weapons: money and power. The Muslims who are at the cutting edge are given a lot of money by clerics to execute their plans. In contrast, the Christian evangelists do not get any financial support.

This knowledge does not seem to harmonize self with self or with the Holy Being. I was struggling to hold myself together. I remembered the song "The Best Book to Read is the Bible." But the Bible is a collection of books. Which book is relevant for me? Job came to mind. As I read the first chapter my attention was drawn to the verse that I had recited at funerals more than a hundred times. "Naked I came from my mother's womb, and naked shall I return; the Lord gave, and the Lord has taken away; blessed be the name of the Lord." I discovered that these are not words for the dead. They are not just for the bereaved. They are the words for those who are being persecuted. They are for those who are experiencing all types of loss: divorce, separation, the death of a loved one. They are for those with reduced paychecks.

As I wrote this memoir I was looking at *Time* magazine, which had on the cover someone holding a paycheck with the question, "Hey, Where's my raise?" Paychecks are shrinking for millions of Americans. The dread is that so many Americans are losing their jobs. Others are overworked with reduced salaries. It is said that some CEOs are becoming richer and richer at the expense of the working class."

So I learned that the Book of Job is not only for me. It is the book for people in the world who experience all types of hardship.

I was using Job's words as food and a weapon. So whenever the spirit of hopelessness and faithlessness knocked at the door, it is answered with "The Lord gave, and the Lord has taken away, blessed be the name of the Lord." I now let go and let God. I remembered the word of the Apostle Paul, "I count everything as a lose because of the surpassing value of knowing Christ my Lord." The Lord graciously restored four great virtues: **faith, hope, love, and joy**. I was being empowered by the beatitude, "Blessed are you when men revile you and persecute you and utter all kinds of evil against you falsely on my account. Rejoice and be glad, for your reward is [not will be] great in heaven [heaven is where God is] for so men persecuted the prophets who were before you." Matthew 5:11.

I now joyfully followed the footsteps of the Blessed High Priest, who, as Hebrew puts it, "… for we do not have a High Priest who cannot sympathize with our weakness, but was in all points tempted as we are, yet without sin." Hebrew 4:15.

I also recalled that those who went before us underwent similar experiences. King David, a man after God's own heart, underwent greater tribulation which is echoed in Psalm 55:12-13.

"If an enemy were insulting me; I could endure it,
If a foe were raising himself against me; I could hide from him.
But it is you, a man like myself; my companion, my close friend,
With whom I enjoyed sweet fellowship;
as we walked with the throng at the house of God."

Yet whatever we were going through, we were fully assured that God is with us. We prayed and believed with the psalmist, "Cast your cares on the Lord and he will sustain you; he will never let the faithful fall." We indeed enjoyed God's presence and surprises.

CHAPTER FOURTEEN:
SUNDRY SURPRISES

Sunday, July 13, was full of surprises. It was my 45th spiritual birthday. The very first thing I did was email my spiritual twin brother Habel to remind him that on this day both of us committed ourselves to Christ. I still remember the scripture that was read of Jesus healing a man at the pool. This man had been sick and waiting for the angel to stir the water for thirty-eight years. When Jesus met him He asked, "Do you want to get well?" Rather than saying yes, the man complained, "Sir I don't have someone here to put me in the pool when the water is stirred up, while I am trying to get in, someone else got there first." Rather than entertaining his complaints, Jesus said miraculous words, "Get up, pick up your mat, and go." This man was immediately healed.

I still remember how I was healed that night. Like the man in the Gospel story, I was not expecting to be healed. I was going to feed my humor. I had heard that there was a gathering where men, women, youth, and children gathered to mention their sins. I was going there to have something to laugh at. But as the Scriptures were read, and people started repenting of their sins, I discovered that it's was not a joke. Thus, that night the precious Redeemer touched my heart. The Holy Spirit convinced me of my sin. I repented and confessed how I cursed God in 1953. The anger was triggered by one of the most critical episodes in my family. It was during the war of land and freedom, commonly known as the Mau Mau Emergency. By this time my father had died of natural causes. On the material day, my mother was taken to the Home Guard camp for interrogation. She was to be there some days without food. My elder sister made githeri (the poorest type of food consisting of nothing but boiled maize). The word githeri means "nothingness" because for the Kikuyu the real food (irio) must have beans or peas and English potatoes and vegetables. For security purposes my sister sent Josiah, who was seven. She avoided sending me because I was big enough for interrogation, which included torture. When Josiah took the food, he found mother being tortured. Yet, instead of thinking about her pain, she told Josiah, "If I don't come back home, you and the other children have to farm at Mwiro." This was our bigger farm. However, after being beaten up, she was released. Gideon, who was five, while I was eleven, remembers a different reaction. Gideon remembers that when we saw our mother weeping and with a broken thumbnail, our first reaction was to take the little githeri she was carrying and eat it because we were very hungry. In my case, I never remembered the little food, I remembered her tears, bleeding thumb, and how I looked at the sky and asked God, "You call yourself Great Provider, Ngai? [Kikuyu name for God] Is this what you have provided for us?" Josiah remembers that while the Kikuyu tortured our mother, it was a military doctor who was a Kamba who gave her treatment. So God miraculously provided for us and protected us since we lived in a battlefield. So in this time of great stress, God was in control and had our best interest at heart. Better still, he was preparing me for the ministry to the Sudanese, who have lived in war and have seen their mothers and fathers die, and their brothers and sisters taken to slavery. That most difficult time gave me an empathetic understanding for the people who had gone through great tribulation. Throughout the years God has proved to be the Great Provider.

I recalled that for forty-five years there has never been a time when I approached God through Christ without experiencing His precious presence. He is a God who is ever present. He is indeed Jehovah Jire (God who provides). As the Kikuyu put it, Ngai ni Ngai, meaning, the Great Provider is the Great Provider.

I start the morning with meditation. I was using Day by Day as a guide. The key words (which I did not notice when I was preparing the sermon for the day are in Amos 7:7: The Lord was standing beside a wall built with a plumb line, with a plumb line in his hand. The author reminded me that God is the builder who uses a plumb line to straighten our lives. Our lives are in the process of becoming God's Temple. The tools that God uses to straighten us include disappointments, demotions, promotions, humiliation, exaltation, pain and comfort, good news and bad news, prayer and meditation, the Holy Scriptures, and the Holy Spirit.

After being illumined and empowered by these words, I went to Southeast Park. It was a two mile walk. I carried a loaf of bread and ugali to feed the birds. It was a bright, sunny, and cool morning. I reflected on the number seven as I walked. I recalled that I was empowered by the seventh verse of the seventh chapter of Amos. On the Sunday that we commemorated our Extravaganza, which was held on the seventh day of the seventh month, we had seventy people in attendance. We gathered seven thousand plus dollars. This is the seventh month of dwelling in a vicarage of a congregation that I don't minister. Is God using this symbolism to convey an important message to me? What is it all about?

While I was pondering this mystery, the Sabbath motif was popping into my mind. I was led to Hebrews, "So then, there remains a Sabbath rest for the people of God; for whoever enters God's rest ceases from his labors as God did from his." Hebrews 4:9-10. I discovered that the number seven is about my Sabbath. Two things are required as a road map for the Sabbath: faith and obedience. "For we who believed enter that rest."

I was now feeling restful as I approached the pond. I spotted the first brace of ducks. They waited for me expectantly. I remembered my favorite morning songs:

> *"Thou Who feeds the birds,*
> *Feed me also.*
> *Fill me with the Holy Spirit,*
> *For He is the spiritual food."*

The ducks now came closer to me. They enjoyed the bread and *ugali*. As they competed for the bread, I remembered a Kikuyu proverb: "That which picks up with its beak doesn't pick for someone else." It is survival of the fittest. Yet even the weak don't go hungry. The Great Provider is so compassionate and so merciful that he cares for even the weakest and tiniest bird. As I fed the birds, I was reminded of two great African sayings: "The plant which is protected by God is never hurt by the wind." And that "A fire which is protected by God is kept burning by banana leaves." Banana leaves are the poorest type of firewood since they don't set aflame. This implies that God will protect you even when you are a lamb among wolves.

When I walked home, I was refreshed and rejuvenated by the pleasant sunshine, the singing and swimming birds, and the green trees. They are all sacramental. Through them I experienced the presence of the precious Being. I was indeed enjoying eternal rest.

After breakfast and meditating on the sermon, I made pastoral calls. I had to call upon my spiritual babies in the same way a mother duck was calling her babies in the pond.

At 1:00 p.m. I headed to the church. I had to pick up Fr. Chris who has no transportation. By 1:30 we were at the church. This gave us ample time to prepare the altar and do anything else that needs to be done. We vested at 2:00 pm... Kim was the first surprise. She is a member of University Church who renders the children's ministry. And then Sunny came, she is a member of St. Peters who also helps in the children's ministry. Both of them are very spiritual ladies; I was surprised to see them because I was not expecting them, in summer the Sunday school teachers were expected to resume in the fall.

There was apostolic disappointment. It was 2:25 p.m. and none of the Africans and Mexicans had come. I had teachers, but no children. There were two priests, but no congregation. But I still believed they would come. Deacon John and Mubure were the first to appear. They are the most committed members. Minutes later there were twenty people, among them seven children. I knew the teachers had a class. I was surprised to see the Williamses. I had called the father that morning and he told me that he would not be able to come because he was working. But I had insisted that he see to it that his children came for Sunday school. His wife is Muslim, but his two children are Christians.

During the announcement Deacon John informed me that Fatuma, who is a Muslim, had made a prayer request. Was that not another surprise? After the service we went to see the artwork that was done by the children. They had done a superb job. I was overwhelmed by the work of Kim and the children.

After church Fr. Chris and I headed for pastoral visitation. We started with the Mexican family. They had not been in church for the last two Sundays. We were met by Omer, a twelve-year-old boy, in the driveway. He ushered us into the living room. Garcia welcomed us warmly. He hugged me firmly to communicate his love. He took to the master bedroom, the only room that had air conditioning. In the room there were three expensive items: a king-size bed, a big screen TV, and a dresser. I congratulated Maria and Garcia for having those items. Maria commented, "Father, this is my first bed. I have always slept on a mat. So when I decided to buy one I had to get the best." Then, Maria introduced her aunt, her niece, and her husband, who had just come from New Mexico. None of them spoke English. Maria assured me that they would join the church. There are now nine people living in a two bedroom apartment.

After introductions and visiting with each other, we had a healing service. We prayed for Zeus who is having problem with his tonsils, Maria's aunt who was being bothered by her uterus, and the niece who was pregnant.

After this we went to see Fatuma, a twenty-minute drive. As she opened the door, she was overcome by seeing two priests. There were things scattered all over. All the seats were covered with clothes. There was virtually nowhere to sit, yet Fatuma was not bothered. She said warmly, "Welcome, Father! Take a seat." She cleared one portion of the couch and a chair for us to sit on. She sat next to me. She showed me her hand, from which she is suffering terrible arthritis developed when she was working at IBP. I laid my hand on hers in the name of God, beseeching Him to uphold her and to grant her healing. Through her faith she was healed. She has a very strong Muslim background. She also has a strong faith in God and his healing power. It goes without saying that the Muslims are a community of faith. The Koran, as with the Bible, associates faith with obedience. It is stated in Sura 2:67-71, "When faith is lost, people are up for disobedience with various excuses: even when at last they obey in the letter, they fail in the spirit, which means that they get fossilized, and the self-sufficiency prevents them from seeing that spiritually they are not alive but dead." Ministry to the Muslims is indeed misio Dei, which is not opposed to misio Christi.

After this we drove to Angelina's. She has been sick for months. When she eats anything she throws up. But she must attend a seven-day-a-week job at IBP. She was asleep. Maikal had awakened her. While she prepared to come to the living room, her husband wanted me to show him how to operate his computer. He in on the Internet but doesn't know how to get into it. After showing him how to get to the Internet, Angelina came into the living room looking frail. She is so tall that I preferred that she sit so I could reach her head. But she felt that she must stand for healing. I had to get on my tiptoes to lay my hand on her head. We prayed for her and she was strengthened.

It was now 7:00 p.m. I took Fr. Chris to McDonald's for supper. I drove to his apartment and then went home. After watching a little bit of TV I felt sleepy. Since I was alone, I bid myself goodnight and had a deep sleep. Glory be to God.

CHAPTER FIFTEEN: CALL TO GLORY

It was late in the afternoon when I received a call from Laura. "Father Chris has died. His body has been cremated. And there will be a memorial service at the Community of Grace United Methodist Church next Saturday. And Reverend Terry would like you to officiate the service with her." I had mixed feelings of sorrow and joy. Sorrow because I knew I had lost a great friend and partner in mission, and a person whose ministry was parallel to my ministry. He had ministered to the homeless. I am ministering to the refugees who are very much like the homeless. Like Christ, I spent many years working with street children who were like a sore to society. Christ was incarnated in the homeless culture. When I was rehabilitating juvenile delinquents who were called children of the dumpster, I was called a dumpster. Thus, I felt that I had lost a companion who could truly empathize with the people to whom and with whom I ministered and me.

I am, however, happy because Chris is in a better place. He is in a realm where he shall hunger no more or thirst no more, and the sun shall not strike him anymore or any scorching heat. He is in a realm where he is totally free. No worry about bills. He is experiencing perfect joy, perfect peace, and perfect love. He is indeed having the Easter experience.

His memorial service was attended by twenty people who were representatives of the society that he had touched. There were the mentally handicapped. Christ had lived with a young man who was mentally handicapped for seven years. He was with this young man until he was taken to a nursing home. There were the physically handicapped. There was a former homeless man who had been Chris' friend for twenty-six years. There were Africans and African Americans. There were CNAs and a registered nurse. Of the two clergy who officiated, one was a lawyer and the other was a doctor of ministry, doctor of religious education, and doctor of divinity. Even though Chris was survived by two sisters, none of his relatives were there. They possibly might not have understood the nature of his ministry.

Terry officiated using the Methodist liturgy, which has a message of death and new life in Christ:

> *Dying, Christ destroyed our death.*
> *Rising, Christ restored our life.*
> *Christ will come again in glory.*

"Wayne's life was all about love," remarked Terry, using 1 John 4:7-21 as a text. "Chris never saw color or class. He embodied the love of God, which embraces all humanity. The story of his life is 'Beloved, let us love one another, for love is of God, and he who loves is born of God and knows God.'"

Mary remarked in her eulogy how we got to know Fr. Chris when were still ministering at University Church, and how her husband got into trouble by asking Fr. Chris to supply for him. She said, "Fr. Chris consistently challenged us to invite everyone to church. His message was, 'Invite everyone to church, even if he is homeless. Help out the homeless and when you do this, don't brag about it.'" She also told the congregation how Chris visited her husband in the hospital when he was hospitalized with pneumonia. The trip to the hospital took Chris took 3 hours (instead of 20 minutes) because he had to use public transportation."

After the sermon, there were remarks from a nurse who works in the VA hospital where Chris was hospitalized remarked that he ministered to the patients until he could not walk anymore. She remembered an episode when, "Chris was weak, his lips were blue. He would not admit that he was too weak to minister to another." A homeless man who had come by bus remarked, "I have known this guy for twenty-six years. When I first met him I was nineteen. We have gone through tough times together. When I was sick in the hospital he visited me every day. He was a good guy."

Chris' ministry was similar to that of Mother Teresa's or St. Francis', who was his patron saint. What a blessing for Chris to be with the Son of Man and to hear these words, "Come, you blessed of My Father, inherit the Kingdom prepared for you from the foundation of the world, for I was hungry and you gave me food, I was thirsty and you gave me drink; I was a stranger and you took me in; I was naked and you clothed me; I was sick and you cared for me; I was in prison and you came to me."

CHAPTER SIXTEEN:
ANGER IS LOSS

It was Holy Week. It was Maundy Thursday when Jesus had the last supper with his disciples and the day that he was betrayed. The sky was clear as I drove on Western Street in Amarillo. I was going to the post office. A Swahili proverb popped into my mind: "Hasira hasara." Anger is a loss. The Spirit of the Lord was using this proverb to counsel me. It also seemed that the Spirit was preparing me for something nasty. This time I found only two letters in the mailbox. Both of them had a diocesan letter head. One of the letters appeared to be a circular while the other appeared personal. I suspected that one of the letters was responding to our request for financial support since I have written a letter to the ordinary (bishop) asking for support. I was wrong.

When I arrived in my office I started with the circular letter. It was from the canon to the ordinary advising the priests and parishes about a diocesan medical insurance. The letter reminded me of how I had been alienated from the diocese. Even though I work eighteen a dozen, the diocesan administration machinery regarded me as a supply priest who is like substitute teacher who is called only when the actual teacher is unavailable.

And for this reason I was not included in a medical plan. This was a punishment I had to endure for planting a congregation while black for the black and yellow, white and red. After I had read the letter, I remembered what the Spirit was whispering to me: Anger is a loss. So I chose not to be angry. I had to suffer without bitterness.

I then opened the second letter. It had come from the ordinary. It was nastier than the one from the canon to the ordinary. The ordinary was ordering me to vacate the University Church vicarage and was direct. He stated that I must move by May. I feel uncomfortable, but not bitter. The Spirit was echoing in me a Swahili proverb: "Anger is a loss."

Worse still, it was in this holy week that I had noticed in the *Journal of the 45 the Annual Convention of the Diocese* that my name was removed from the list of the parochial priests and was now listed under "non-parochial resident clergy." The senior warden, who had become my Judas and had deserted us, is listed as the leader of St. Cyprian's. As far as the Diocesan Center was concerned, I was both nonparochial and unsalaried. The devil was using this devise to deflate me before the great mission.

As I was visiting my fellow priest for comfort, I found him having a conversation with his staff. They all seemed to turn cold shoulders to me. I deduced that they were having a malicious gossip.

When they were done I told the rector that I would like to see him for a few minutes. "Yes," he responded. We then moved to his office. He said, "I wanted to visit with you to communicate a message from the vestry." He was throwing his ball to me before I threw mine. That was his opening statement. I knew exactly what he had to communicate. It was about our children. A few weeks before they had turned a wheelchair into a toy and had broken its wheel. We had talked about it, but now the vestry had discussed the matter. He told me that the vestry has asked that the children be supervised. "This is not a request. It is an ultimatum. Children must be supervised," he commanded with a loud voice. Or as we say in Kikuyu, "Kwaria ta kiri ruunguini." After apologizing I told him that I would do my best. I didn't want to promise that this would never happen again. I know on Sunday we will have Extravaganza and

I was expecting a large number of children. Some children come without their parents and it is difficult for anybody to control them. The ones who had broken the wheelchair were unaccompanied by parents. But there is something in Abuna and Mama Mary that attracts children to them. This is of course the love of God, which the spirit has shed in our hearts.

I felt humiliated, yet I refused to be infuriated. After being reprimanded, I told the rector that I wanted to know if we could have our own telephone line. Up to this time, my cellphone was the official telephone of St. Cyprian's. At first he told me that they couldn't afford another telephone line. I told him that we would be paying the bill. He then told me that he would take the matter to the vestry.

Even though I felt I had a jeremiad, the word of the Lord advised me not to be angry. I was reminded of Proverbs 16:32: "He who is slow to anger is better than the mighty, and he who rules his spirit than he who takes a city."

After the incident the devil laughed at me and tried to convince me that I was somewhat too soft. But the Spirit reminded me of the scripture, "A soft answer turns away wrath; but a harsh word stirs up anger." Satan retorted with the words from Ephesians 4:26, "Be angry." But the Spirit reminded me that the devil is taking the Holy Scripture out of context. The word of God is actually saying, "Be angry but do not sin, do not let the sun go down on your anger, and give no opportunity to the devil." The devil intended to be enthroned and to drain spiritual energy before the special event. He also knew that I had a flock that was hurting. He wanted me to turn to myself rather than concentrating on the divine activities inherent to Holy Week.

What would Jesus do? Or rather what would Jesus say? He could say, "Thy will, and not mine, be done." He could also insist, "You have heard that it was said to the men of old, 'You shall not kill; and whoever kills shall be liable to judgment. But I will say everyone who is angry with his brother shall be liable to judgment, whoever insults his brother shall be liable to the council." So the Spirit of the Lord reminded me, "Hasira hasara."

After the office work I drove home. I had to prepare for Maundy Thursday's Eucharist and foot washing service at St. Paul's in Dumas. At 5:00 p.m. evangelist John Nyaga and I were in a Toyota Camry. As we were driving, the Spirit of the Lord urged me to visit with Maria's family. Arriving there I found Gonzales, her twelve-year-old son, sitting in the van. He was sobbing. "What is going on?" I asked.

"My mom is in jail."

"When did this happen?" I asked with a low tone.

"The police have just picked her up."

While we were still talking his eleven-year-old sister came to me. Tears were flowing from her eyes. Her beautiful face had turned red, her eyes swollen. She came and leaned on my breast as she was sobbing. I embraced both of them. I was moved with compassion to the point of shedding tears. Garcia, Maria's husband, came out. He looked desperate.

"Father, I am trying to be strong, but I can't. Maria had a long day. She had just come from the dentist. She sat in the dentist chair for two hours. And just a few minutes after arriving home, the police came and took her to jail."

"What had she done?" I asked.

"It is alleged that she fought at her workplace. But I don't know what to do. I don't know how much they will demand for bailing her out."

I was moved with compassion. We held our hands together and asked for a miracle. I prayed that this family might be strengthened. After comforting and encouraging them, I gave them the small check that was intended to help them buy food for Extravaganza and I told them to use it for bailing Maria out. The incident of 1953, when my mother was tortured by the Home Guards, gave me an empathetic understanding. I knew what it meant to have the breadwinner confined. After the prayer we started driving to Dumas, north of Amarillo.

The sky was very dark, indicative of torrential rain or hail. After driving a few miles it was pouring heavily. The road was hazy. But I didn't want to give up.

I was still feeling pain for Maria and her family. Their suffering doesn't compare with the bad tidings that I had received. The family had lost the breadwinner. This was not the first time. The husband was feeling helpless. It was now down to me why the Spirit gave me strength. I was being equipped for this vital ministry. Besides, I needed the peace of God, which passes all understanding, to be able to drive in a heavy rain.

By 6:55 p.m. we were at St. Paul's Church. The service had to start at 7:00 p.m. It was quite unusual for me not be at the church thirty minutes before the service. And for that reason, this lovely and loving congregation was very concerned. We spent five minutes talking about the weather. But I still needed a few minutes to go through the bulletin since this was my first Maundy Thursday with them. Francis had already prepared the bulletin. I went to check the place where we performed the foot-washing ceremony. I had to adjust a few things. But since the very meaning of the word liturgy is the work of the people, I opted not to change the liturgy.

To my surprise there was a high degree of participation. When I was performing the foot washing, Francis was reading the anthems for me. This was new. It was indeed spiritually nourishing. I was sanctified by these words as I was kneeling and washing and wiping the feet.

The Lord Jesus, after he had supped with his disciples and had washed their feet, said to them, "Do you know what I, your lord and Master, have done to you? I have given you an example that you should do as I have done."

"Peace is my last gift to you; my own peace I now leave with you; peace which the world cannot give, I give to you."

"I give you a new commandment: Love one another as I have loved you."

The peace of God was being fueled by Jesus' words. "I have given you an example that you should do as I have done." Those words were summoning me to abide in the servant ministry, a ministry to those who are in prison, the families of the prisoners, the refugees, the poor, the mentally ill and the homeless, and the overworked and underpaid. As I minister this category of the people of God, the Lord Jesus is giving me the last gift, peace. I would not trade this gift for anything. With this gift I can smile at the storm. Remember, I am not saying smirking at the storm. I am saying "peacefully smiling at the storm."

The ritual of "undressing" the altar and the removal of all the icons from the sanctuary was powerful. All the members participated in this activity while the lay reader read Psalm 22 with a sadness that expressed the pain of Jesus on the cross I was strengthened by the following verses:

"My God, my God, why have you forsaken me?"
Why are you so far from me,
"And so far from the words of my groaning? (22:10)
Do not be far from me,
 For trouble is coming (10, 11)
All the end of the earth will
Remember and turn to the Lord."
"And all the families of the earth will bow before him,
For dominion belong to the Lord
And he rules over the nations." (27)

What David and our Lord Jesus went through was more painful that what I was going through. Jesus say the cross as glorification and as a way of drawing all nations to him. Being blamed for a lack of civility of immigrant children didn't compare with the pain that the mother of our Lord had to endure as she heard her son being misjudged by the very people who were waiting for his coming, and him being whipped by the very people he had come to save, and him being hung on the cross by the very people he came to redeem, and him dying for the crimes which he did not commit. Yet God exalted him to the highest place and gave him a name that is above every name in heaven and on earth and under the earth and every tongue confess that Jesus Christ is Lord, to the glory of God the Father."(Philippians 2:9-10). I now realize what I went through was a preparation for the ministry that God has entrusted to us as Patriarch of All Nations Christian Church International which is an association of Churches and Ministries in over seventy countries.

CHAPTER SEVENTEEN:
MESSAGE IN A DREAM

READ THIS ONLY IF YOU are interested in the message in dreams or if you are a student of analytical psychology. Morton Kelsey has rightly contended that, "If...humankind is open to another dimension of reality, then the dream may be one of the most common avenues through which God reaches out to us."

I was up at 4:00 a.m. to finish writing the above chapter. At 8:00 a.m. I was tired and sleepy. So, being on vacation, I decided to go back to bed. Then I had a dream. I saw myself walking down an avenue with many trees. I was also meeting people of many races. As I was walking, my shoe became too tight and uncomfortable. I decided to go to a special store where I could get a special pair of shoes. On the way I met a white lady who seemed to read my mind. She told me that she knew I was looking for special shoes and that I can get them in the import store. I went there and found the shoes I was looking for. As I was walking to church, I reached the spot where I had left a pair of shoes and I found many pairs of shoes there. Reaching the place where I had left a pen, I found hundreds of pens. There was now a group walking with me to church. I picked one pen and told those who were walking with me to pick up the pens if they so wished, because they were free. After passing the avenue with trees I reached a bridge. As I was crossing the bridge I saw a Muslim lady I had been trying to win for Christ. Her husband and children are baptized. I was surprised to see her going to church ahead of me because she never came to church if I did not called her on Saturday. Now she is ahead of me. We went on and reached the church. In the church there was a gigantic bed. Being tired I slept right in the middle of the bed. To my surprise I saw many children sitting at the edge of the bed. One child, who was sleeping with his mother and close to me, started edging over to where I was sleeping. He eventually discovered that I was sleeping in the nude. He reported to his mother that the priest was naked. Then the mother checked to find whether that was true. When she found that I was naked, she reported it to everybody in the room. Then the children started singing in unison in Swahili "Padre u uchi." The priest is naked. One child who was near my head modified the song and sang "The priest is naked because he is very tired." I pulled on my pajamas and dressed while covering myself with the blanket. The incident was so humorous that I was awakened by my laughter. Mary, who was sleeping with me, asked why I was laughing. When I narrated the dream, she said, "I can't interpret your dream. But I got a message from your dream. We have so many children in our church, every adult member of the church must participate in the children's ministry." We then decided that after my vacation, Mary will meet with all the women and I will meet with all the men to talk about the children's ministry.

My interpretation:

In my dream journal the shoe symbolizes moving. The dream is predicting that we are going to move from the church where we have been worshipping for one and half years. I had to also move from the vicarage where I have resided for seven and half years. I am to undergo two rites of passage. The rites of passage, as Van Gennep observed, are not without crisis. The pen symbolizes education. I have a tremendous job of educating my congregation. Besides learning English, they have to learn civility. Interestingly, 95% of the members are students.

Nudity symbolizes crossing the culture and going far beyond the tribal norms. It is a sign of being incarnated in many cultures. So I am a pastoral tribe, a legal and an undocumented Mexican immigrant, a native American, a black American, and an Anglo. Their pain is my pain, their crosses are my crosses, their vulnerability is my vulnerability, their joy is my joy, their generosity is my generosity, and their free spirit is my free spirit. Seeing myself in the nude also symbolizes fear of poverty. The price that I had to pay for the ministry to new immigrants and refugees is the loss of compensation. As I was seeing in this dream, I will eventually be financially abased and my family and I will be without medical and dental coverage for many years, yet there was divine protection. I was physically and psychologically and spiritually healthier than ever before.

The house symbolizes self. I have given my very self to this international and interracial community. They have also given themselves to me. They are in me, I am in them. They are a part of my archetype. This is why their shortcomings are my shortcomings. Their strength is my strength.

Amazingly, this dream was prophetic. Five years later, Bishop Doyle and I went on a mission to the Sudan. We spent six days in the cathedral compound in Duk. I was moved to tears when I saw that this was the spot I had seen in the dream, and the children and youth I had seen in my night vision. I was dumbfounded to have seventy youth staying with us at night. They were very spirited and had composed songs to comfort, encourage, and affirm us. Most of the time they did not fall asleep until after midnight. They talked loudly and their voices were like the sound of many waters.

About the nudity. You may think that the dream was spicing it up. Not at all. Bishop Doyle, who was also the symbol of a padre, a manna person, and the holy man, had to sleep and take baths outside in view of the natives.

In my case, I had to wash in a small booth that was adjoined to the cathedral compound. The door was a blanket. The children and other people in the compound could see my naked back. If someone had come to the latrine that was next to the booth, he could see the remaining part of the padre.

As noted, nudity is a symbol of the fear of poverty. Unfortunately, our host perceived us as Americans with inexhaustible financial resources and so they persistently asked us for financial assistance. By the time we left Duk, we had no money for incidentals and we had a real fear of being destitute. By the time we were in the Juba airport to fly to Kenya, we were destitute bishops who had to beg money for the transit visa to Kenya. But as you will see later, the Lord miraculously came to our aid.

Interestingly, the child in the dream who perceived that I was exhausted was predicting what happen to my companion immediately after we arrived in Duk. Bishop Doyle suffered heat exhaustion. As in the dream, he found understanding men and women who fanned him and wet his head and shoulders, and kept him cool. We were both ministered unto. We experienced compassion and the love of God. We, indeed, saw the face of Christ in Dukan Christians.

Predictive dreams, as it is with prophecy, are fulfilled in portions. This dream was fulfilled in part when we were cast out of the Episcopal Church. While we had freedom of Spirit, there was the fear of poverty since there was no regular stipend. Yet, we never felt alone since we belonged to a great multitude that no man could number, from every nation, from all tribes and peoples, and tongues. Standing before the throne and before the Lamb, clothed in white robes, we had come out of great tribulation. The good news is that at the end of all things, we will hunger no more and not thirst anymore, and the sun shall not strike us, nor any scorching heat. For the Lamb in the midst of the throne will be our shepherd, and he will guide us to springs of living water, and God will wipe away every tear from our eyes.

CHAPTER EIGHTEEN: FUNDRAISING BANQUET

WHEN THE CHURCH RECEIVED COMMUNICATION from the bishop that the diocesan funding would cease in July, it resolved to hold a fund raising banquet on July 6, 2003. This date marks the anniversary of the first Extravaganza, which was held on July 7, 2002. In Kenyan symbolism, seven seven (Saba Saba) symbolizes the second liberation, the date when the majority of Kenyans were liberated from the oppressive KANU party, which had usurped all power and had become the judiciary, the executive, and the parliament. This was the date when a multi-party system commenced. With regard to St. Cyprian, this was a liberation of the cultural ethos, which entails celebrating our diversity by singing in all languages represented, and eating cuisine of all the participating countries.

The church committee planned to employ the African method of fundraising. Each working member had to give $25. This money had to be brought first and then the names of the contributors would be read out. I had to bring the contributions from my friends. Our guests were given an opportunity to give.

We started the program with uplifting music. We sang in English, Swahili, and Dinka. This was followed by a homily based on Matthew 25:14-30 and Malachi 3:6-11, which went as follows:

GIVE YOUR BEST

Both Malachi and the parable of the talents are telling us to give our best. In the parable Jesus is challenging us to be adventurous. Most of us here are adventurous and have the experience of thinking out of the box. We enjoy listening to people who are different from us. You know that those who look different and talk different increase our understanding of self and of the world about us. The parable tells us that God gives people different gifts, that the reward of work well done is still more work, and that the person who gets punished is the person who never tried. But more importantly we are challenged to give.

MALACHI challenges us to give our very best. Do not give to God what you cannot give to your governor. Do not give to God a polluted food, a blind and lame animal. If you do that, God will not be gracious to you. If you do that, God will send a curse upon you.

BLESSING

If you give generously to God and bring the full tithes, the Lord has promised that He will give all kinds of good things. He will not let insects destroy your crops. The Lord will open the window of heaven for you. He will pour down for you overflowing blessings.

The sermon was followed by a presentation from Simon. He gave the brief history of St. Cyprian's and how we started as a home church. Then, welcomed by the Community of Grace United Methodist Church, we first called ourselves the African Community Church. Subsequently, we chose St. Cyprian as our patron saint and named the church St. Cyprian's International Church. After that he highlighted how we received a communication from the bishop that the funds for clergy compensation would cease the end of July. This is why we were holding a fundraising banquet.

Josiah Mwithiga and Maikil Mandwat stood to explain the fundraising method. Josiah informed the participants that we would use the Kenyan method of fundraising, which was initiated by the late president Jomo Kenyatta. We would start receiving money that was collected from the members. This would be followed by donations from the guests. And during the banquet, the congregation would be informed about the amount that was collected.

As people were feasting, Josiah and Maikil brought good news. Josiah informed us, "You have done a good job. We have collected a lot of money. But we have a wrong figure and I cannot mention the figure until it is corrected. We have to give more money." So we went on giving and Josiah kept on saying that we still had a bad figure. It was less than $7000. We finally got the right figure: $7060. This was a lot of money for St. Cyprian's since the average Sunday collection is $65.00.

Do you see what I am seeing? Do you perceive a unique number? Is this number accidental? Is there a divine message? We are in the seventh month. We are celebrating the first Extravaganza, which took place on the seventh day of the seventh month. We are now feeling that the holy figure must be seven thousand. For your surprise there are other sevens. The diocesan support will be ending in the seventh month. Without being redundant, as I write this memoir I am in the seventh month of my stay in the vicarage adjoined to St. George's without being vicar of St. George's, and living across from the university where I used to be a chaplain. Yet I have nothing to do with chaplaincy. I am here, yet I am not here. I am in the womb. There are two more sevens that symbolizes my genesis. I was born on the twenty-seventh day of the seventh month.

And I was born again on July 13, 1958. This was the most magnificent day of my life. It was the day that I repented of my sins and committed myself to Jesus Christ. I recall this great day was preceded by untold tribulation in the Kikuyu land, which was commonly known as the Mau Mau Emergency. Those were the times when the Kikuyu were fighting for their lands and freedom. More than 200,000 Kikuyu perished. I still remember seeing five dead men as I was going to school. Those were men I had revered as my fathers. I was so scared to see them dead. Our homes were burned. We were hungry and most nights slept in the bush. Our mothers were beaten. We were terrorized by the Mau Mau at night, and the British Army and Home Guards during the day.

So, the vicarage, even though it is a desert, is nothing compared to the dreadful years of the Mau Mau Emergency. As the Lord brought great light to our country after great distress, I believe the vicarage desert was a preparation for greater achievement and freedom. For now, the vicarage was a desert, a wilderness of meaninglessness. I had been here now for two months without a family. As I write this note I am alone. I do not know why the Omniscient has kept me here. Is the Loving Being giving me a sabbatical? I do not know, but it is more than likely. For six years and three months (this is not an accidental figure) I overstretched myself most of the time, working sixty hours a week. By the end of this period I was feeling so tired I was longing for a sabbatical. But the Being who has all knowledge and wisdom had given me a sabbatical and wanted me to dwell in the same home. The Holy Spirit had called me to this desert. Yet, there was a miracle of manna for St. Cyprian's and me. The Great Provider who fed the Israelites in the wilderness, fed seventy people who had attended the banquet. And I could still hear Jesus saying, "Gather up the fragments that remain, so that nothing is lost." He had also preserved my family.

There is still another seven. Five years later, St. Cyprian's International Church birthed All Nations Christian Church International, which now has ministries and churches in over 70 countries with over two million members. To my joy-filled surprise, ANCCI was chartered as a not-for-profit corporation in the state of Texas on July 27, 2007, and was granted a 501C (3) by the federal government the same day. Among our churches, we have a Messianic Congregation that cerebrates Shabbat every week. They have fellowship and have their meal with gladness. This reminds us that as Christians we are called to enjoy God's rest. Therefore, since the promise of entering His rest still stands, let us be careful that none of you will fall short of it. We enter His rest by faith in and obedience to God, attending church every Sunday, and by honoring God with our time, treasure, and talents. "So let us make every effort to enter the rest, so that no one will fall by following their example of disobedience." Hebrews 4:1, 11.

CHAPTER NINETEEN:
IN GOD'S TIMING

It is God's timing. Our time is in His hands. He moves us at His own good time. He uses numbers to reveal his mystery of accuracy of timing. He comes at the opportune time. This is why he wants us to believe and say with the psalmist: "Trust in the Lord, and do good; so you will dwell in the land and enjoy security. Take delight in the Lord, and he will give you the desire of your heart. Commit your way to the Lord; trust in him, and he will act." Psalm 37:4-5. For five years we have been struggling to own a dwelling. Today we are waking in our own home.

Yes. On the 5th day of the 5th month of 2004, my family enjoyed the first morning in a new home located at 70 Hunsley. Note that Hunsley has seven letters. Is the Lord telling us that we have to forgive seven times seventy? Yes. There are people we have to forgive. We have to forgive those who have misjudged us, those who have spread false damaging allegations against us, and those who have bought into malicious gossip and made wrong decisions, which have hurt my family and me. We have to forgive the old Judas. We have to forgive the new Judas. We have to forgive those who had only utilitarian relationships with us and who deserted us in the most difficult times.

In this great morning, as we thank God for the new day, someone popped into our minds. We are recalling a grandson who was born on the 5th day of the 5th month of 1995, weighing 5 pounds and 5 ounces.

We recall that his mother was born in 1975 when her mother was 25 years old. We recall that his grandmother was born on the 25th day of the 12th month in 1950. Paying attention to number five, the mother and the grandmother of this boy have exactly the same number of 5s. We note that while the mother has 1975, the grandmother has 1950+25=1975. According to Kikuyu symbolism, 5 represents new birth. Traditionally, when a baby boy is born, the women report the birth to the father with five ceremonial ululations, which is very much similar to alleluias.

The message behind God's timing is profound and unfathomable. We cannot fully understand what is behind the numbers. But we are fully convinced there is a message. It may be that God is leading us to a new dimension of ministry. The Ancient of Days is moving us from grace to grace, and from glory to glory. We may face new challenges, but there are new opportunities as well. We feel led by the peaceful cloud. Word of the Being is a light unto our paths. We tenaciously hold his promises: "And I will lead the blind in the way they know not, in the paths that they have not known I will guide them. I will turn the darkness before them into light, the rough places into a level ground. These are the things I will do, and I will not forsake them." Isaiah 42:16.

CHAPTER TWENTY:
AWESOME EXPERIENCES

On March 9, the first Sunday in Lent, I had three surprises. I had just pulled into the parking lot and realized I had forgotten the key to the church. It takes an hour to return home to fetch the key and by the time I would have returned everybody would have left. I was, however, astonished to see Deacon Rose Ann. She assisted me on the first Sunday of each month. But this was the second Sunday of the month. She greeted me with "I don't know why I am here." I told her that she was there to open the door for us because I didn't have the key to the church. I also knew that the two daughters were not there to read the lessons. So Rose Ann helped us to open the church and to read the lessons. She was indeed sent by God. During the service she guided the children to their Sunday school class. Shepherding these children was just like herding rabbits, but Rose Ann enjoyed it.

The second surprise was twenty-one-year-old Zenobia, a speech major at West Texas A&M University. She was the only African American who took advantage of my pastoral canceling skill when I was chaplain at the university. Hundreds of African Americans had promised to attend either the Canterbury or the church, but never fulfilled their promises. But Zenobia never failed to keep her appointment. Unlike other African women, she doesn't put chemicals in her hair. Her hair is as natural as mine. She has tirelessly endeavored to organize black women students. She is strong enough not to allow male students to take advantage of her. In retaliation they have acted ugly toward her. One morning she found a snow penis at her door. She has been a victim of character assassination. During the counseling session, which was marked with tears, I helped her identify her personality type. She is an ENFJ and read in my book about her personality type. "You are for sure an ideal group leader, collaborator, persuader, motivator, participant, nurturer, humorous, caring, concerned, magnanimous, trustworthy, influential and empathetic." (Githiga, Initiation and Pastoral Psychology page 162)

She learned that she could be a good clergy person, performing artist, or apt teacher. Pastoral counseling helped her to know herself better, and to understand why her character was being attacked. After counseling she promised me that she would become Anglican.

I am now delighted to see her sitting in a pew. She is not going to receive communion because she is not baptized. We have scheduled her baptism though.

After the service Zenobia told me that she felt dumb. The Anglican liturgy is unfamiliar. I told her that it is all right to feel that way and that eventually she will be edified by the liturgy.

We had thirty-one people in the church. After the service we had to attend a thanksgiving party at Mabure's home. It was the 40th day after the birth of Deng Mabure Ding Mabure. The main focus, according to Deacon John, was the Mother. We were praising God for the successful delivery.

After the service Mary, Isaac, and I drove to the Mabure's. As usual we were given the best seats. To our complete surprise, the gathering was interfaith and international. There were thirty-one people, the same number, but different people from those who attended the church. Women prepared the food. Most of them had not come to church. There was a relaxing atmosphere as we were conversing and listening to Arabic music.

Deacon John, who lives with Mabure, told us how the neighbor called the police on them. She calls if their guests park in her spot or if they make any noise. He recalled an incident. They had come home past midnight after work. They turned on the water to prepare the tea. Suddenly, there were policemen knocking at the door. Outside there were paramedics, firefighters, and a police car. They were all there because the exhausted brethren turned the water on in the kitchen.

We didn't want to dwell on the negatives. So we shifted gears and started discussing our diverse cultures. We talked about the naming system. The Muslims told us that they are named after the prophets, such as Musa and Mohamed. The Dinka people are named after their parents and grandparents. The name deposits the history of the people in such a way that a Dinka using the names can trace his roots up to twenty generations. This is why the newly born have four names.

Before dinner Deacon John called the people to order. He prayed in Arabic and read the Bible and gave a homily in Arabic. I prayed in Swahili. We then enjoyed the delicacies. As we were driving home at 6:00 p.m. Mary and I felt relaxed and energized. We praised God for calling us to this ministry and for finding us worthy to minister to many nations and an interfaith community. We are most grateful to the Ancient of Days for fulfilling the words of his prophet Micah through us: "In those days…many nations will come and say, 'Come, let us go to the mountain of the Lord, to the house of God of Jacob; He will teach us His ways so that we may walk in His paths. Nations will not take up sword against nations, nor will they train for war anymore.'" Micah 4:1-3. We were indeed experiencing the short term fulfillment of this prophecy. We enjoyed revitalizing ourselves in the diversity of cultural ethos.

CHAPTER TWENTY-ONE: SUNDRY BLESSINGS

ON MARCH 16, 2003, THE second Sunday in Lent was marked with surprises of the Holy Spirit. We had planned the blessing of the marriage of Rocio and Carlos. But they had a fight two weeks before this day that resulted to the cancellation of the ceremony. I paid them a pastoral visit and Rocio stated that she doesn't want to be married anymore, and they are not now talking to each other even though they still live together. Carlos had not come to church for a month.

So instead of the wedding we have the holy baptism of Deng Mabure Ding Mabure — the first born of Mabure and Amir. In the morning I had called Mabure to remind him to be at the church at 1:30 p.m. "Please don't be late," I insisted. I had also called Carlos and asked him to come to church.

Mary and I were to drive two cars. Mary had to pick up Gladys, our Sunday school teacher.

I had to pick up Kim, an acolyte, and June, a lector. We were at church on time.

The first surprise was that all the participants were on time and I had time to rehearse with the acolytes. When I went to the parish hall to call the members to church, I heard a voice. "Dr. Githiga, you pretend that you are not seeing me. Why are you ignoring me?" Turning, I saw that it was Zenobia.

"I am sorry," I responded apologetically. She expressed her forgiveness by giving me a hug. This is her third Sunday in the church.

Since most people are new to the Anglican liturgy, we started by going through the baptism service. I instructed the parents and the sponsor how to stand and what to say. Customarily, a Dinka couple does not sit together in church. So it sounded weird to them for Abuna to tell them to sit together and stand together during the presentation. After this preparation we started the service.

During the baptism, fifteen children came to the font to witness the baptism. They were unusually well behaved. The baptism was crowned by ceremonial ululation. Then we sang "I have decided to follow Jesus" to dismiss the children for Sunday school. The adults remained for a homily and inquirers' class. When I was half way through the inquirers' class, I was astonished see Carlos and Rocio and their children entering the church. I quietly praised God for bringing them to church. This would have been their wedding day. But thanks be to God they are together in God's house. Is this not the work of the Spirit of the Risen Lord? He who said, "Those who are well have no need of a physician, but those who are sick. I came not to call the righteous, but sinners" Mark 2:17.

During the announcements we had more surprises. We started by welcoming the newcomers. There were two brothers from Sudan and I asked Mangar to introduce them. "I am not going to introduce them," Mangar responded. "Let them introduce themselves." The two men stood and introduced themselves. They said they were astonished to see a congregation where the majority of the members were Sudanese. They promised to become members. They were applauded. Simon then asked me to reintroduce Zenobia. After introducing her I asked her to say a few things about herself. The congregation was jubilant to learn that she is African American and that she would be baptized on Sunday. She is the first black American to be a member of St. Cyprian's.

Simon then told me to introduce Carlos because he had not been in the church for a long time. He also whispered, "What about their wedding?"

"Let's not talk about that," I whispered back.

Then Carlos stood and introduced himself using limited English. To our surprise he said, "Next Sunday will be my birthday. I will bring a birthday cake." He was applauded.

After the Eucharist, we went for refreshments and for the celebration of the birthday of Agor, Simon's daughter. I sat with Carlos and Rocio and their children. After visiting with them I asked Carlos to visit me tomorrow for counseling. He agreed that he would come. He also told me that he had decided to quit his job as a bartender, which was luring him to alcohol. As I was talking to them, I was looking from the corner of my eye at a lady with her little girl. They were sitting by themselves. I asked Carlos and Rocio to excuse me so I could visit with them.

"I am glad that you worshiped with us today. I am Father John," I said as I introduced myself.

"I am Melody."

"Tell me a little bit about yourself," I said.

She responded, "I am a stay-at-home mom. I come from a big family. We were four sisters and four brothers. I like to stay home to take care of my children. I was so surprised today to see an infant baptism for the first time. I'm a Baptist and in our church we don't have infant baptism. And so what I saw today was a great surprise."

William and Nada were another surprise. Nada is a Muslim and has never shown any interest in becoming a Christian, while William and his two children are baptized in the Anglican Church. William had stayed home for several months without coming to church. So I called him Sunday morning and told him how we have missed him. He told me that he could not come since he was working, but will send the kids.

To my surprise William came with Nada and their children. I had a digital camera but didn't have a photographer. I asked William whether he would take pictures for me. He responded with a beautiful smile and said, "Sure."

Jorge Gonzales and Maria Teresa and their children were another blessing. They came to church for the first time three Sundays ago. I had visited them and they assured me that they had decided to become members of our church. So I called them in the morning and told them how we have missed them. Jorge told me graciously, "We are coming, Father." I was so delighted when I saw him with his family.

CHAPTER TWENTY-TWO:
MEETING WITH ORDINARY

MAY 15, 2003, WAS THE day that Mary had to leave for Kenya for a two-month vacation. Four weeks before this date we were busy with preparations. We had to buy things to take to my mother, mother-in-law, sisters, brothers, nephews, and nieces. These necessities, the airline tickets, and money for incidentals left us without any cash flow. While our accounts were depleted Rehema, our daughter, was hit by an uninsured drunk driver. Her car was totally demolished. Praise God she had no broken bones. The police officers, who came to the accident scene, wondered how she was still alive. She had to go to the hospital for a medical checkup. She had no health insurance and lived on a tight budget. We had to assist her with the towing expenses. When it rains it pours. We were left with no cash.

A day before the departure Mary worked nonstop. She had to see to it that a lady would coordinate Sunday refreshments at St. Cyprian's when she was gone. She had also to see to it that Isaac and I had enough food for two months. I tried to discourage her from this work, but it was as if trying to force a fish not to swim. She had to be the best mother and wife in absentia. She went on and on until midnight.

On the day of departure she woke at 7:00 a.m. and by 8:30 a.m. we were in Amarillo International Airport. We found Rehema, who worked at the airport, waiting at the ticket counter. Looking at her I perceived something was wrong, but she didn't want her mom to know about it. While Mary was busy talking with her nephew Benson, Rehema whispered to me that Mary's tickets were not found in the computer. "But don't let mom know about this. I have talked to the manager and he is working on it." After 45 minutes the itinerary was computerized. Rehema also arranged that her mom be treated as a VIP and be assisted by someone with a cart in all the airports. All that she had to take care of was her passport and tickets. After her two suitcases were processed we escorted her to the departure gate. We then gave her a goodbye hug and headed to Canyon.

As we were driving I reflected on how Mary had given all her heart, mind, and energy to the new church and her family. She didn't have enough time for herself. Yet the Lord was taking care of her. I remembered the word of the Apostle Peter: "Cast all your cares upon him, for he cares for you."

MEETING WITH HIS GRACE

I had not informed Mary that I had an appointment with the bishop. Somehow I was sensing disappointment. It was now six and a half months since the bishop visited with me. After meeting with the bishop's committee, he informed me then that he had decided to appoint me as a missioner to St. Cyprian's Church and I would start work in January 2003. I would continue to reside in the vicarage. He further told me that there were funds for six months.

I had, however, good news to share with the bishop. The church had been increasing in number. We had at least five new members every month. While we had existed for only thirteen months, we now had a Canterbury program for the students attending Amarillo College that included four Bible study groups: junior acolyte, senior acolyte, and two adult Bible study groups. One adult study group concentrated on Mexicans, while another concentrated on Africans. We hold bimonthly Gospel Extravaganzas in which we celebrate our diversity by praising God with all languages represented, and then we enjoy international cuisines. This momentous event brings Muslims and Christians together. We also had a strong Sunday school program headed by Jo Snead of St. Peter's Episcopal Church. We had Sunday school teachers from St. Peter's and St. George's. They were all godly Anglo Americans.

The uniqueness of the congregation lays in the fact it is the most integrated and fastest growing in the diocese. It also is a wedge to the Muslims. African Muslims regard Mary and me as their spiritual leaders. They call us whenever they have crises. Some come to church for healing prayer.

So I have so many things to share with the bishop. I am meeting with him in his apartment at the Diocesan Conference Center. I knocked on the door and the Bishop opened it. He appeared different. I made a comment about his beard and his weight loss. He told me that his host served him food with little or no meat and that he was feeling much better. He then offered me a glass of water.

After this I started sharing with him about the ministry. He appeared apprehensive. There was neither a word of appreciation or encouragement. After sharing the story, he told me that the reason for the appointment was to inform me that there would be no compensation for me after July, and that he is giving me this information as a brother so that I could adjust my budget. He would be able to provide $100 per service, which is the mount given to a retired supply priest. This meant reducing the compensation from $57,955 a year to $5,200 a year. He advised me to apply for a job elsewhere outside the diocese.

I was horrified to note that he did not show any interest in the ministry of St. Cyprian's Church. After his decree, I quoted a scripture that I was meditating on:

And I will lead the blind in the way they know not,
In the path that they have not known I will guide them.
I will turn the darkness before them into light,
The rough place into level ground.
This I will do,
And I will not forsake them.
Isaiah 42:16

After this the bishop closed our meeting with prayer.

The encounter with his Grace raised more questions than answers: Why does the bishop have nothing for me in the diocese? Has someone poisoned the well for me? Has someone put me on the street? Does the bishop really understand the model of my ministry? Why am I being penalized for implementing the Diocesan Mission Statement which reads: "The diocese…will provide the energy, resources, and support necessary to help all our communities become mission outposts and where needed, to help plant new ones." Why abandon the newest mission while other missions that have existed for decades were still being supported? Are the Africans not a part of the Anglican Communion or of one holy Catholic Church? Are the members of St. Cyprian's excluded from "a great multitude that no man could number, from every nation, from all tribes and peoples and tongues?" Why do we recite in our liturgy:

"Let not the needy, O Lord, be forgotten
Nor the hope of the poor be taken away."
Why do we sing:
"In Christ there is no East or West
In him there is no South or North,
But one great fellowship of love
Throughout the whole wide earth."

Metaphorically, I felt like a hen that was being separated from her newly hatched chicks, or a soldier who is in the battlefield and receives information from the command in chief that his supply will be cut off. I indeed felt alone and lonely. The dream that included nudity was fulfilled.

What shall I say? Why the priests? Are buffaloes not more collaborative than the priests? When hunted by a lion the buffaloes team together to defend the weak. They are determined to die in defense of the feeble. Why am I in the holy orders, which at this time is most unholy institution on the planet? Was it not religious leaders who plotted, arrested, and handed over Jesus of Nazareth to be crucified?

MEDITATION

Even though I was wounded, I couldn't start the day without meditation. After a long silence, the Holy Being led me to the word of the prophet Isaiah: "

You are my servant, I have chosen you and cannot cast you off, Fear not, for I am with you. Be not be dismayed for I am your God; I will strengthen you. I will help you. I will uphold you with my victorious right hand." Isaiah 41:10.

Powerful are these promises. The Great Provider is reminding me that he is the one who has called me, not the bishop. He has chosen me and he will give me unfailing support. The Omniscient is also revealing himself as the Faithful Witness and the Righteous Judge. He has a word for my accusers:

"You shall seek those who contend with you, but you shall not find them; those who war against you,

shall be as nothing at all, For I, the Lord your God, hold your right hand. It is I, who say to you, "Fear not, I will help you." Isaiah 41:12-13.

At this time the key words are: "You shall seek those who contend with you, but you shall not find them." I am remembering those who orchestrated my removal. I recall that the storm was triggered by an abundance of visions that the Lord had given me. The major vision was the establishment of a preschool program that would use the spacious vicarage, and would also allow the vicar/chaplain to purchase his own dwelling. I had researched and found that the average stay of a vicar/chaplain was four and half years. I learned that the primary reason for this is housing. I am one of the two priests who stayed the longest. The diocese had not taken steps to care for the chaplains through housing.

To my complete surprise, I was their cherished priest until I started purchasing a house. The Church was one of the fasted growing churches in the diocese. The idea of a black chaplain owning a dwelling ushered in the campaign of personal destruction and character assassination.

However, the word of God is powerful. And not one iota of it will not be fulfilled. It was and is being fulfilled in my eyes. Those who contended with me are nowhere to be found, even though I still dwelt in the vicarage that was adjoined to their sanctuary. They indeed have no power over me. The guardian angel is protecting us day and night.

Nevertheless, I am still enraged. I am torn between the attitudes, "Lord forgive them for they know not what they are doing" and "When evil doers assail me, my adversaries and my foes, they shall stumble and fall." I am still too devastated to concentrate on "For I, your Lord, your God, hold your right hand, it is I who say to you, fear not, I will help you." I struggle to sing with the psalmist, "The Lord is my light and my salvation, whom shall I fear? The Lord is the stronghold of my life, of whom shall I be afraid?" As powerful and affirmative as the words are, they are not answering the question: Why should evil, arrogant, and selfish people prosper while the righteous suffer? Why am I suffering for tireless dedication to misio Christi? Why did I bother to implement the diocesan vision statement, the vision of the National Church of 2020, which encouraged doubling the membership by the year 2020? Why was I so foolish as to not distinguish rhetoric from reality, the walk from the talk?

After being invaded by these endless questions I turned to the devotional books. I opened *The Stream in the Desert* by Mrs. Charles E Cowman. "My expectation is from Him," Psalm 62:5, is the theme of the day. I am particularly enlightened by these words, "Every prayer of the Christian, made in faith, according to the will of God, for which God has promised, offered up in the name of Christ, and under the influence of the Holy Spirit, whether for temporal or for spiritual blessing, is or will be fully answered." These words are now like a sunbeam shining in the dark night of my soul. I remember that in the forty-five years that I had walked with God, there has never been a time or a minute that I approached him with faith that I did not experience his gracious presence. God is gracious, which is the very meaning of the name John. I was praying and owning the promise of "Fear not for I am with you." I am experiencing his sweet quality. He is indeed, with, by, and in me. His comfortable promises I now possess: "For I the Lord your God, hold your right hand, it is I who say to you, fear not, I will help you."

The Lord has put a new song in my heart: "The best book to read is the Bible. The best friend to have is Jesus." "The Lord is my shepherd; I shall not be in want."

CHAPTER TWENTY-THREE: DEPARTURE FROM THE EPISCOPAL CHURCH OF THE UNITED STATES

FOR SEVENTEEN YEARS WHEN I ministered with the Episcopal Church, I learned that three things were most valued: buildings, money, and numbers. All other things, evangelism, and pastoral ministry were secondary. The clergy of a parish having a magnificent church building and the most affluent members were greatly rewarded financially. Those who reached out to "one of the least of these my brethren" were devalued. I was becoming a liability by reaching out to the poor immigrants. Thus the diocesan funds were to be saved from the clergy who were wasting time with a nonfinancial generating community.

The following letter from the bishop that he wrote after our meeting underscores the point.

Dear John,

I simply want to reiterate the details of our conversation at my apartment on May 15. As we spoke about then, the diocesan funding simply will not be able to provide the full stipend for you for the last of this year, and I am not sure how much will be available in calendar year 2004, but I doubt seriously it will be a full funding of stipend.

As I said at that time, I believe we can assist the congregation with paying the $100 per service supply as you continue to serve them, and we will send that directly to the congregation and they can pay you out of their operating fund... During that visit I also told you that I will be willing to contact other bishops nearby should they have positions that might suit your gifts and abilities. I am in the process of writing that letter to those bishops now and hope that they will be in touch with you soon.

Even though we have had a fruitful ministry of the international and national communities at the university, His Grace was convinced that I could only minister to the Africans. It never dawned on him that Africans have diverse cultures. So he wrote to his fellow bishop stating in part:

Dear D,

I write to recommend to you the name of a priest who may well be valuable to you as you begin to reach out to 70,000 African immigrants now living in the Houston area of which I heard you speak recently. The Rev. John Githiga is a priest of the Diocese of Northwest Texas who originally comes from the Anglican Church of Kenya. In his younger days he began full time ministry as a catechist, later being ordained deacon and priest. John has been in ECUSA for 20 years, attaining a D.Min from Sewanee several years ago. He has been in a mission in Canyon and chaplain to West Texas A&M in Canyon for 7+ years. Last year he resigned to work with a group of newly arrived African immigrants in Amarillo. The diocese agreed to stretch to pay his salary for the first six months of 2003, but unfortunately we do not have a resource to continue a full package for Father John.

Father Githiga can provide you with his full C.V. and any other information you may desire. I believe with a large number of immigrants in Houston area, he may well be able to build up the Episcopal Church in the area in a way that might take several years to do in NW Texas.

In this letter the bishop is falsely stating, "he resigned to work with a group of newly arrived Africans." I didn't resign. I was phased out for planting a new congregation, in keeping to the diocesan mission statement and the prayers in Anglican Prayer Cycle. The vision of planting a church was not an either/or, but both. The mission only added more ministries to Mary and me. We had three congregations: University Church, University, and St. Cyprian's Church. The campus parish included teaching New Testament studies, being president of the United Campus ministry, a yearly picnic of international students in our backyard, weekly student lunches and fellowship, and individual counseling. The University Church included weekly Sunday services, Wednesday services, and regular parochial ministries. St. Cyprian included the activities mentioned earlier. The ministry to the immigrants was in obedience to God's call of reaching out to the persecuted church. I did not intend to do it alone, but wanted to engage the people of God who included university students and the members of the University Church and other churches in the area. We were also obeying the Great Commission, "Go therefore and make disciples of all nations." All nations included Africans, Mexicans, African Americans, and Anglo Americans.

The grievous mistake that the bishop made was that he never consulted with the university community or St. Cyprian's congregation.

The latter endeavored to visit with the bishop but he declined. For the seven years we ministered, God always provided the funding because it was His mission. We never had any problem of paying all our bills, including diocesan apportionment. There was a financial blessing in both the University Church and the diocese. But when the ordinary resolved to withhold support from the voiceless, the diocese was negatively affected. The bishop's letter highlights this point.

Dear Friends in Christ,

I am writing you about a matter of deep seriousness that is challenging our diocese. As I am sure you are aware, many members of St. Nicholas Episcopal Church in Midland have left both St. Nicholas and the Episcopal Church to form a congregation that aligned itself with a diocese in Uganda. St. Nicholas paid none of the apportionment for the first five months of 2005, a sum amounting to just under $50,000. Their total apportionment of $109,000 will not be paid in full. Those who chose to remain with St. Nicholas Episcopal Church do not have the resources to pay this sum...In addition, a $10,000 shortfall from other sources includes the now-defunct St. Cyprian's congregation in Amarillo. This has put the Diocese of Northwest Texas in a difficult financial condition. Not only are we in a cash "crunch" for the present, it appears that without help from individual members of the diocese, our situation will continue to deteriorate.

Ironically, by trying to save money from an "African" priest, the bishop lost two congregations to the African bishops and the financial situation in the diocese "continues to deteriorate."

Led by the Holy Spirit and my conscience, I resolved to pull out from Episcopal Church USA and align with the Anglicans.

As it was in the case of so many faithful and orthodox clergy who were called out of the Episcopal Church, I was served with a Letter of Inhibition. The notice of inhibition was sent to the presiding bishop, recorder of ordinations, secretary of the house of bishops, all the bishops of the Episcopal Church, and clergy and vestries of the diocese. The letter stated in part:

> *"This is to affirm the determination of the Standing Committee of the Episcopal Diocese decision, pursuant to the provisions of Title IV, Canon 10, Section 1 of the Constitution and Canons of the Episcopal Church in the United State of America, that John Githiga is inhibited from the right to exercise the gifts and spiritual authority as a Minister of God's Word and Sacraments conferred on him in ordination and is further inhibited from exercising any other priestly functions beginning January 26, 2005, for a period of six months."*

THEOLOGICAL REFLECTION

AT THE PERSONAL LEVEL, THIS letter was not a surprise. I had been served with a directive that sounded like "If you take that route you will see it." I had also visited with other faithful clergy who had received the same whip. I had visited with Father Chuck Filiatreau whose parish had transferred its canonical residence to the Anglican Diocese of Thika, Kenya. Chuck and Gretchen gave me a right hand of fellowship. As I was struggling to find where to go, Gretchen insisted, "I know where you can find a good bishop."

"Where," I asked.

"Thika," she responded. As I unconsciously repeated the same litany, Gretchen interjected, "I know who is a good bishop for you."

"Who is he?" I queried, as though I didn't know whom she would recommend.

"Gideon."

Gretchen was right. I knew Gideon as a brother and also as a clergyman who had gone through fire with his ungodly bishop for being a type A priest.

Gideon also has a tripartite theological heritage, with a B.D. from St. Paul's United Theological College, Kenya, an STM from General Theological Seminary, US, and a PhD from Oxford University, UK. He is, of course, more educated than my inhibitor. And so I took Gretchen seriously.

St. Cyprian's and I asked for canonical residence in Thika. By the time I was inhibited, I had moved from ECUSA. St. Cyprian's was one of five parishes in the United States under the oversight of Bishop Gideon, and one of hundreds of parishes in the United States and Canada under the oversight of African bishops.

By divine design, the Letter of Inhibition came to me while I was hosted by Father John and Mother Ruth Urban who had received the same notice. These godly ministers of the Gospel prayed with me and comforted me. They indeed had empathetic understanding.

As we reflected on the unChristian practice of claiming power to take away the spiritual gifts of a servant of God, we learned that it drew from the feudal system during the Dark Ages, whereby if the landlord laid his hand on you, you became his property. So the said church employed this inhumane and undemocratic system for the clergy who parted company with them. In my case, the system was not applicable, since I was not ordained by the bishop of the said Church. I was ordained by Langford Smith, bishop of Nakuru of the Church of the Province of Kenya. It can also be argued that had I been ordained by the bishop of the Episcopal Church, it is unscriptural for any human being to claim the authority of taking away spiritual gifts. Spiritual gifts are God given. As the word of God puts it: "There are varieties of gifts, but the same Spirit, and there are varieties of service, but the same Lord, and there are varieties of working, but it is the same God who inspires them all in every one."

During the ordination, the community and the bishop authenticate something that is already there. The Kikuyu word for ordination is gukunura, meaning "to remove the lid and let it flow." In traditional religion it was believed that if God called someone to be a priest or a prophet, he had no choice. If he refused the ordination, he would suffer calamity after calamity until he removed the lid so that the prophetic gifts may flow.

According to the Biblical accounts of the calls, calling is God's business. It is something that is designed by God before birth. As the Lord said to Jeremiah: "Before I formed you in the womb I knew you, and before you were born I consecrated you, I appointed you to be prophet to the nations." Jeremiah 1:5. It is God who calls, equips, and sends. And for that reason there is no creature, not even the angel of light, with the power to take away the gifts that God has bestowed on us. Our gifts flow from the Being who transcends all that is seen (and unseen) and who has power over all that he has created. And thus for another human being to attempt to take away the spiritual gifts, is very much like trying to pump water from the ocean to drain the ocean. Or as the Kikuyu say: "It is like grinding water with grinding stone." (Kuhura mai and ndiri). Attempting to take away spiritual gifts was like fighting fire with petrol.

It gave me increased energy and desire to reach out to all the people of God, people of all nations and all social strata. Our ministers included people like Father Chris who ministered to the homeless. And because of that, though he was Anglo and Anglican, he could not qualify to minister with the Episcopal Church.

Interestingly, most of the clergy who were inhibited by the said Church are mightily used by the Holy Spirit. They have brought many souls to the Kingdom of God. All glory to God. Amen.

CHAPTER TWENTY-FOUR:
ON THE EDGE OF A CLIFF

I HAD A DREAM IN which I saw myself walking alone on a hilly road. As I was climbing, I got exhausted and laid down because of weariness. I was frightened to see the edge of a steep cliff at my right hand. As I was lying just a few inches from the cliff, I was petrified when I saw a sixteen-wheeler truck coming toward me. I had a dilemma. I had to choose between moving to my right side and falling into the abyss, or remain lying where I was and be run over. I opted to remain lying down. I thought the driver would see me and stop, but to my disappointment he didn't. So I felt the truck running over me, and I was amazed that I was not hurt. I then woke up peacefully.

This dream was a graphic expression of my feelings toward the ministry among the Somali. I never had any dealings with them when I was in Kenya. Here in America I had met a few of them, but had no connection. I heard many horror stories about them. That they are opportunists, liars, parasites, and shrewd. Two Somalis can work using one Social Security number. I have heard that they are all 100% Muslim and would never become Christian. As a matter of fact, I had never seen a Somali Christian.

I had already had disappointing experiences with the Sudanese. They asked me to help them start a church and I spent countless hours with them. I worked hard to get them scholarship aid. We got going-back-to-school materials for their children. I got them an English teacher. We gave them orientation to the American way of life. But when I fell sick with pneumonia and lost diocesan support, we were forsaken for greener pastures.

Now I am facing Somali Bantu. I had been reading about them. I knew that 210 families of Somali Bantu were expected to arrive in Amarillo. How did I connect with Somali Bantu? Accidentally. I was visiting a refugee neighborhood on South Austin when I met Abdi's family. They had just come from Kakuma, Kenya. Abdi spoke Swahili. None of the members of the family spoke either Swahili or English, but we quickly connected with Abdi. The connecting threads were that we were both Bantu, spoke Swahili, and had Kenyan experience.

After visiting Abdi several times and bringing groceries to the family, he introduced me to two other families. My invitations to come to church with me were not successful. Instead of coming with me, he opted to babysit the children of three families so that two mothers could come with me to church. That day I had four Kenyans and two Somalis in the van. The Somali ladies were wearing headscarves and long dresses. They looked like typical Somalis. One of them spoke Swahili, the other one didn't speak English or Swahili. We started with supper and then praise music, followed by Bible study. When I took them home, all the children were waiting for them outside. They were jubilant to see their mothers back home.

I started visiting the Somali Bantu more regularly. I took their youth, together with the Sudanese and Congolese, to the youth program that included games, food, and Bible lessons. Unlike other Africans, the Somali youth were insulting. One of the kids told me in Swahili as we were approaching the church, "Mzee, wajua kwetu ni dhambi kuingia kanisani?" (Old man, do you know that it is a sin for us to enter the church?) When I was driving them back after feeding them, the young man complained about the van. "I never enter a vehicle without music."

Despite their negative attitude, I decided to concentrate on one family, Mama Mnose and her grandchild Husain. I prayed with them and took Husain, who was sixteen, to church. I gave him an English-Swahili New Testament. I read the Bible with him, and he also read alone. But for him to accept Christ was, as it were, a matter of life and death.

Nevertheless, the dream, as with visions and prophecy, had an immediate message for me, the worldwide church, and countries like the United States and Kenya, both of which received Somalis. It is estimated that more than fifteen thousand Somali have migrated to America and European countries. There are a large number of Somali in Kenya. They all have one thing in common: They don't integrate with the society. The message for the church is that we must study the history and the culture of the Somali. We have to find out why they don't easily accept the Gospel and why they don't assimilate.

After studying the history of Somaliland, I learned that there was a small number of Christians in Somalia. Ironically, most of the Christians came from the Bantu, which is a minority ethnic group evangelized by evangelicals and the Wesleyan Church of the Nazarene. There is one Roman Catholic diocese for the whole country, the Diocese of Mogadishu, which at one time was estimated to have 100 members. During the early colonial era, there were virtually no Christians in Somalia. And even those who later became Christians were orphans from church schools and orphanages.

When the civil war started, the missionaries left without raising educated pastors. Eventually the Islamic militia confiscated all Christian schools and churches. Not only that, there were no church buildings and no legal protection for Christians. The jihadists label Christians "Ethiopian intelligence." And for that reason, they killed all Christians in Somalia. Mnasuur Mohammed, a Somali Christian, was beheaded by Sunni Muslims while they were reciting the Koran. Western and

African missionaries who sacrificed themselves to feed the hungry were murdered. In November 2003, a Kenyan Christian working for Seventh Day Adventist Mission in Gedo, South West Somalia, was murdered by Islamist radicals. The attack appeared to be deliberately anti-Christian and anti-Western. In the same year, a British couple, Richard and Enid Eyeington, working for SOS Children's Villages in Somaliland were shot dead by gunmen in their home inside the school compound while watching television. Worse still, they hunted Somali Christians in neighboring countries such as Kenya and Ethiopia. A story is told of a Somali Christian living in Kenya, who was tranquilized and taken to Wilson Airport (a small private airport) and flown to Somalia where he was murdered.

Thus in Somalia, Christians are regarded as apostates from Islam who should be killed. In February 2003 a radical Somali Islamist group, Kulanka Culimada based in Mogadishu, issued a press release in which they called for all Somali Christians to be treated as apostates from Islam and killed.

It suffices to show why, in the dream, I saw myself lying helpless between a sixteen wheeler truck and the abyss. The dream had a message for me personally, for the worldwide church, and for the global village. The message for me was that I could not reach the Somalis single handedly. It is not a ministry for a lone ranger Christian. It is a ministry that calls for the corroboration of many Christians. These should be a team of people who are funded and who have to study the history and culture of the Somalis and other Islamic countries. The wealthy churches need to fund these teams that are at the cutting edge.

It is reported that in Kenya there is a Samaritan group that is reaching out to Somali Christians. These and other ministers who are preaching the good news in Islamic countries need the support of the worldwide church. The wealthy Arab countries are funding their brothers in building mosques, Islamic colleges, Islamic newspapers, and Islamic think tanks. Christians should do better in supporting their own missionaries. This is the message for the West, which is receiving Somalis as refugees. It should know the price they will have to pay. They need to love and befriend their children and youth. Since Somalis do not integrate with other children at school, they are bullied, and this makes them indignant against the host country. This is a challenge, too, for teachers who can hold a friendly discussion with Somali students. A story is told of a concerned teacher who held friendly discussions with Somali students. They discussed Al-Qaida and their training cells. The teacher was surprised when the students told her that they knew their websites. She asked them to show her the websites on the school computer, but since school computers filter those types of the sites, they could not get them. The teacher took them to a computer outside the school and the students showed her the websites.

If you are a Somali Christian or if you are a believer within a harsh Islamic environment, be assured that you are not alone. Greater is He who is in you than the one who is in the world. Being a patriarch of churches and ministries in more than seventy countries, I know the Christians who are being persecuted in North America, Europe, the Middle East, and Africa. We have a word of encouragement for you. The most encouraging words come from the Book of Revelation, which was written by a suffering pastor to the suffering church. He refers to himself as John and says, "…your brother and companion in suffering for the kingdom with patient endurance that are ours in Jesus." The Risen Lord revealed seven great blessings. But we must perform seven acts:

1. *We must see the glory beyond the present suffering.* When Jesus was facing the cross he prayed: "Father, the time has come. Glorify your Son, that your Son may be glorified." See yourself as conqueror. Our Master said: "In the world you will have trouble. But take heart! I have

overcome the world" John 16:33. Moreover, Paul assures us: "In all these things we are more than conquerors through Him who loved us. For I am convinced that neither death nor life, neither angels nor demons, neither present nor future, nor any power, neither height nor depth, nor anything else in all creation, will be able to separate us from the love of God that is in Christ Jesus our Lord." Romans 8:37-39.

2. *We must bear the cross.* To bear the cross implies that we have to be faithful and obedient to God no matter the cost. We must suffer with Christ that we may be glorified with him. We suffer with Christ because we are God's children. I like the way St. Paul puts it: "The Spirit himself testifies with our spirits that we are God's children. Now if we are children, then we are heirs—heirs of God and co-heirs with Christ, if indeed we share in his sufferings in order that we may also share in His glory." Romans 8:16-17.

3. *We must rekindle the first love.* Remember how you used to have time for fellowship with God and the people of God? How you used to put God first in all things? The word of the Risen Lord for you is: "You have forsaken the first love. Remember the height from which you have fallen! Repent and do the things you did at first. If you do not repent, I will come to you and remove your lamp stand from its place. Revelation 2:4-5.

4. *We have to be faithful till death.* Don't be scared of what you are about to suffer. God will be with you even in the valley of the shadow of death. He will clothe you with peace, which passes all understanding. He did that to thousands of his faithful servants. He encouraged Bishop Polycarp when he was asked to deny the Lord's name. He courageously said to the killers, "Eighty and five years I have served Him, and he has done me no wrong. How can I deny my King who saved me?" The persecutor broke into the house of Andrew Kaguru, a lay reader who succeeded my Father. They demanded that he deny Christ. He courageously responded, "I cannot deny Christ. What you want to

do, do it quickly." They chopped him to death, and he went to glory. There was nothing more they could do to him after that. He was far beyond their reach. Therefore, my dear brothers and sisters, "Stand firm. Let nothing move you. Always give yourselves fully to the work of the Lord, because you know that your labor in the Lord is not in vain. I Corinthians 15:58. If you are faithful only when there is sunshine, you cannot enjoy the victors' promise.

5. *We must not engage in sexual immorality.* No sodomites or fornicators will inherit the Kingdom of God. The Seer put it this way: "But the cowardly, the unbelieving, the vile, the murderer, the sexually immoral, those who practice magic arts, the idolaters and all liars- their place will be a fiery lake of burning sulfur. This will be the second death." Revelation 21:8.

6. *We must watch and prepare for Christ and keep God's commandments.* We must have oil in our lamps. We must "strengthen what remains and is about to die." We do this by reading the Bible every day and participating in Christian fellowship and worship. And by honoring God with our talents, time and treasure.

We must live each day as though Christ is coming today.

We must love God and man and all God's creation. Our Lord Jesus Christ gave the summary of the Law: "Thou shall love the Lord your God with all your heart, and with all your soul, and with your entire mind. This is the first great commandment. And the second is like unto it. Thou shall love thy neighbor as yourself. On these two commandments hang all the Law and the Prophets." When we keep God's word, the Lord promised: "I will keep you from the hour of trial that is coming to the whole world to test those who live on earth."

7. *We must stop being lukewarm.* You may be like the church in Laodicea the seer wrote about. "I know your deeds, that you are neither cold nor hot. I wish you were either one or the other! So because you

are lukewarm—I am about to spit you out of my mouth..." This is one of the dangers of materially wealthy churches. Laodicea was one of the wealthiest cities in Asia Minor. What do you get with material wealth? You need to commit yourself to prayer and immerse yourself in things spiritual and give generously for the mission. Heed the words of St. Paul: "Never be lacking in zeal, but keep your spiritual fervor, serving the Lord." Romans 12:11.

When you stay in the vine and practice piety and are the doer of the Word, all the promises to the seven churches belong to you. There is a precious affirmation in God's word. The Lord's promise is:

1. *You will be given the right to eat from the tree of life.* Unlike the Garden of Eden, fruit of the tree in the City of God is edible. The tree is on the bank of the river of water of life, which flows from the throne of God. It bears twelve fruits and its leaves are for the healing of nations. Right now there are many Christians who are eating from the tree. If you are one of them, you know that you bear the fruits of the Holy Spirit, which are love, joy, peace, patience, kindness, goodness, faithfulness, gentleness, and self-control. You are also aware that you drink the living water every day. This being the case you enjoy the fulfillment of Christ's promise, "Whoever drinks the water I give him will never thirst. Indeed the water I give him will become a spring of water welling up to eternal life." This water can be illustrated with the testimony of a skinhead who committed himself to Christ during KAIRO prison ministry. His head was clean-shaven. His body was still covered with pornographic tattoos. He was two days old in Christ. He stood and said, "I have taken all kinds of drugs, which have put me high in different ways, but I have never been as high as I am this weekend. I had planned to kill some people after my release. But now, I plan to go and give them my testimony." Like the skinhead, when we eat of the tree of life, we attract people to Christ. They drink the living water and pass the same to others, and thus the water continues welling up into eternity.

2. *You will not be hurt by the second death.*" Revelation 2:11. If you continue being in the True Vine and drink the living water, the first death will open an endless, joyous relationship with God. Jesus put it this way, "I am the resurrection and the life. He who believes in me will live, even though he dies, and whoever lives and believes in me will never die." John 11:25. Christ proved this promise by raising Lazarus from the dead. Better still, by being a victor, we will be given glorified bodies. For that reason we don't fear death for "Death has been swallowed up in victory."

We can therefore ask with Paul, "Where is your victory? Where, O death is your sting? The sting of death is sin, and the power of sin is the law. But thanks be to God! He gives us victory through our Lord Jesus." I Corinthians 15:55-57.

3. *You will be given some of the hidden manna.* If we remain in the vine and continue to bear fruit of the Spirit, not only will we be unhurt by the second death, we will be given the hidden manna and "a white stone with a new name written on it, known only to him who receives it." Revelation 2:17. Those who have allowed the Spirit of God to fill every fiber of their being enjoy this blessing. They have inner contentment that cannot be put in words. Paul refers to the gifts when he says, "Contentment and godliness *is* a great gain.*"

4. *You will be given authority over the nations.*" Revelation 2:26. In All Nations Anglican Church we are foretasting this precious gift. I am awed by the authority that the Risen Lord has given the bishops who minister with us. They have the authority to invite my team and me to minister to their nations. I was thrilled by the authority vested in Bishop Stephen Vellaester by his community. During the medical mission, which took place in the dumpsite, the bishop brought together local medical doctors, military doctors, dentists, and student nurses from the local university who ministered to over six hundred patients. He even

asked the military to give the poor boys haircuts. He ordered my team to provide medical facilities. And we all became brothers through service. The Lord has given us authority and power. Is this not what our Master means when he says: "All authority in heaven and earth has been given to me? Therefore go and make disciples of all nations. And surely I am with you to the very end of the age?" Matthew 28:18-20.

5. *You will be dressed with white and your name will not be blotted out of the book of life.* This is another outstanding promise to the victors. They will be dressed in white. White is the liturgical color for Easter. They will enjoy eternal Easter. Thus, whatever you are going through for your testimony and obedience to God, be assured that you are among the great multitude in white robes. This is what John writes about them: "After this I looked and there before me was a great multitude that no one could count, from every nation, tribe, people and language, standing before the throne and in front of the Lamb. They were wearing white robes and were holding palm branches in their hands, and cried out in a loud voice:

> *Salvation belongs to our God,*
> *Who sits on the throne,*
> *And to the Lamb!*
> Revelation 7:9-10

Not only will you worship God in white robes, our loving Savior promises, "For he who conquers I will never blot out his name from the book of life, but will acknowledge his name before my Father and his angels." Revelation 3:5.

6. *You I will be made a pillar in the temple of God and you will never leave it.* After receiving authority over the nations (that is, you have an insatiable desire of giving and receiving from Christians of your own

kind and those who are not your own kind) you will be made a pillar in the temple of God. You are one of the stones in the building. That is, you are a part of the Church Militant and Church Triumphant. We never give an excuse for not attending church. When you go to Church, you don't leave the church with dirt, but with particles of gold. If you are a layman, you are fully convinced that your presence is as important as is the priest's. Your attending the church doesn't depend of feeling, because you are a pillar of the temple of God. If you continue fighting the good faith of faith, you will enjoy what our Master has promised, "Him who overcomes, I will make him a pillar in the temple of my God. Never again will he leave it. I will write on him the name of my God and the name of the city of my God, the New Jerusalem, which is coming down out of heaven from my God, and I will also write on him my new name." Revelation 3:12.

7. *You will be given the right to sit on throne with Christ.* Revelation 3:23. "To him who overcomes I will give a right to sit with me on my throne, just as I overcame and sat down with my Father on His throne. Revelation 3:21. This promise has been realized by the saints who went before us. It is being realized today by those who are still fighting a good fight of faith, and it will be culminated when Christ returns at the end of time. The saying is sure: "If we suffer with Him; we shall also reign with Him." Thus whatever you are going through, realize that you are in the hands of Him who is and who was and who is to come. He is the Being who transcends time and space. Like the psalmist we sing:

> *I lift up my eyes to the hill*
> *Where does my help come from?*
> *My help comes from the Lord,*
> *The maker of heaven and earth.*
> Psalm 121:1

Whatever you are going through, remember you belong to Christ and your life is hid by God in Christ. Listen to His comforting words: "My sheep listen to my voice; I know them and they know me. I give them eternal life, and they shall never perish, no one can snatch them out of my hand. My Father, who gave them to me, is greater than all; no one can snatch them out of my Father's hand." John 10:27-29. When you are at the valley of the shadow of death, shout to the enemy: "The Lord is my light and my salvation, whom shall I fear? The Lord is the stronghold of my life of whom shall I be afraid? When the evil men advance against me to devour my flesh, when the enemies and my foes attack me, they will stumble and fall." Psalm 27:1-2. Do realize that the enemy will use an economic crisis in the family to attack your soul? In the three incidents when we were laid off by ECUSA because of our faithfulness to the Gospel and obedience to God's will, funding was employed as a weapon. But our great surprise was that we never became homeless. We were never naked or without food. Thus, the more the enemy used that weapon, the more we realized that Ngai ni Ngai. That is, the Great Provider is the Great Provider. When the devil takes all your money, use Psalm 23 as your weapon: "The Lord is my shepherd, I shall not be in want. He makes me lie down on green pastures, he leads me beside the still waters, he restores my soul, and He guides me in the path of righteousness, for his name's sake. Even though I walk in the valley of the shadow of death, I will fear no evil, for you are with me, your rod and your staff, they comfort me." Even when you see the shadow of death, don't think that you are going to die. Be fully convinced that God is on the throne and that he has your interests at heart. God indeed watches over the preachers' wives who go through suffering with their husbands.

CHAPTER TWENTY-FIVE: PREACHER'S WIFE

Like Sarah, Abraham's wife, Mary follows me wherever God commands me to go. She not only goes with me, she also fully participates in mission. When persecution comes, she tends to be hurt the most. Being more traditional than I am, she is more hurt by the departures. Being also one of the most hospitable ladies who I know, she is more hurt when economic hardships strike. I have always been surprised by her nurturing and hospitality. Astonishingly, on several occasions Mary begged to have something to give. One of the places she begged was a retirement home where she worked. They had more doughnuts than they could consume. She was given the leftovers for her Sudanese, Congolese, and Mexican children. But what made her a saint was when she suffered depression, she was laid off. When she got better, she went back to the same home to beg doughnuts for her international children. Interestingly, the children believed she owned a doughnut factory. The Cuban poem below describes Mary's hospitality.

> *My hands are empty.*
> *They always give*
> *When there is nothing to give.*
> *Oh, but what is to be done*
> *They are the only hands I've got.*

During our ministry with the Episcopal Church, she participated a lot. Besides being the pastor's wife, she was in the choir, Cursillo, Kairos, Stephen ministry, Daughters of the King, and Women of Vision. She has high expectations of herself and her husband. She is very concerned about my private and public image.

At St. George's and West Texas A&M University, she hosted a weekly women's Bible study that met in our home. She participated in a weekly United Campus ministry that met on campus while I was the president. Every semester she hosted an international students' picnic that was held at our backyard.

In the diocese, she was on the Cursillo staff and participated in the Fourth Day (weekly reunion group) and Altreya (monthly meeting of Cursistas in the northern part of the diocese).

Additionally, she exerted her energy in giving pastoral care to the African refugees, Mexican immigrants, and Native Americans who constituted the membership of St. Cyprian's International Church. She was indeed loved and honored by the people she ministered to and with.

Nevertheless, being a child of lights, she has faced hostility from the children of darkness. When this time comes, I often remember a lesson she read when she was nine years old in a family service at St. John's Church in Nakuru, Kenya. Little did I know that the message she read in Swahili was her message. And little did I know that she would be my wife and that together we will be called to work in the vineyard. She read from Isaiah:

I will sing for the one I love about his vineyard:
My loved one had a vineyard on a fertile hillside.
He dug it up and cleared it of stones and planted it with choicest vines.
He built a watchtower in it and cut out a vine press as well.
Then he looked for a crop of good grapes, but it yielded only bad fruits.
Isaiah 5:1-2

What injured Mary was that the vineyard yielded the opposite of what was expected. As you can see in the previous pages, she exerted all her energy working in the vineyard, and for seven years she didn't have to worry about a means of subsistence. She had built relationships with women of the church, women of vision, Daughters of the King, and Cursistas. We had hospital and dental coverage, and adequate income. She was a mother of two congregations, one of which was predominately white, while the other was predominately black. The majority of the Africans were Sudanese, who are the darkest people on the continent. She enjoyed using her gift of nurturing and feeding. Said differently, she was the fertile soil and the choicest vine she read about in Isaiah. She would also tell you that her husband was a "fertile hillside," who exerted all his energy on the ministry. In most cases, when I was laid off by Episcopal congregations, there was no one to fill his shoes.

But the events that led to our departure from the Episcopal Church were extremely painful. The most painful episode was when I got a call from the rector of the Episcopal Church, which had hosted St. Cyprian's Church, who gave us the information that we could no longer use their facility. We had only two days to move our office furniture and to call the members to inform them that we could not use the church they had been using for two years. I had to quickly move the furniture and jam it in our house. We called the members we could reach and told them to come to our house on Sunday for the service. To our great disappointment none of the members came. They all forsook us and went for greener pastures. We had to start all over again. Now we had no stipend, no facility, and no health coverage. When it rains, it pours. Being my best friend, Mary is wounded by my hurts. While I was not depressed (praise God because someone had to take care of Mary), I was mixed up.

On Saturday, a day after moving the furniture from St. Peter's, there were two events scheduled, both very dear to me. There was a Cursillo staff meeting in Lubbock, of which I was a member. Mary and I had revived this renewal movement in the Episcopal Church. So even though we were being persecuted by the ungodly, we knew there were saints we sought to encourage and nurture. But on this day, there was a hospice banquet where Mary was being honored for her ministry to the sick and the dying. Somehow, I decided to go to Lubbock. Driving from 4th Avenue toward Interstate 27, before I reached the interstate, I remembered that I had forgotten my wallet and driver's license. I returned home and decided to go with Mary to the banquet. The program included encouraging music and a delicious meal. I was encouraged to see Mary receive an appreciation certificate from the ecumenical body. But I was still confused. After the program, I found myself in the women's restroom (toilet). It dawned on me that I was in the wrong place when the next-door neighbor had female shoes. I had to finish up as quickly as possible and get out.

At this time we had to do whatever job we could get to have a means of subsistence. It was hard for Mary. She had lost the children who looked up to her. She had lost her spiritual partners and her friends. The women who had attended Bible study in her home did not come anymore. The family had no medical coverage. Mary had so many unanswerable questions. What shall we do if one of the family gets sick? How shall we pay the bills? What if my husband dies, who will take care of his remains? Where is everybody? These questions resulted in depression. There came a time when we felt alone and lonely. At this time we could say with Apostle Paul, "At my first defense, no one came to my support, but everyone deserted me. May it not be held against them! But the Lord stood at my side and gave me strength, so the message might be fully proclaimed and the Gentiles might hear it. And I was delivered from the lion's mouth. The Lord will rescue me from every evil attack and will bring me safely to his heavenly kingdom. To him be glory forever and ever." 2 Timothy 4:16-18.

As with Paul, God stood by our side and gave us strength. I still remember what God did for us on the Tuesday following our expulsion from the Episcopal Church facility. My head was spinning as I visited Pastor Darren Dye of Freedom Fellowship Church. I shared my story with him. He then prayed for my head and I was instantly cured. He then prayed that the very first telephone call I made would inform me where my congregation would worship on Sunday. I went home with spiritual energy and called Rev. Kenneth who promised that he would pray for us. Thirty minutes later Kenneth called and told me, "John, I have a church which will host your congregation." This was the Christian Heritage Church (which is a Holiness Church). When we met with Pastor Gary, we made an agreement that we would pay $100 to the caretaker, and clean up the sanctuary once a month. For the last seven years St. Cyprian's has been worshipping in CHC. God is Jehovah Jaire.

While Mary enjoyed a large sanctuary, she lost most of the spiritual children, the Sudanese, Congolese, and Mexicans. Being Wakibisi (a Swahili word for refugee meaning "they who keep on running away"), they ran away for greener pastures. The Lord brought a few Anglos, Native American Christians, and Kenyans. Four Native Americans and one Anglo participated regularly. These lovely Christians joined us in reaching out to the children. We even reached out to the children of the parents who left us for that greener pasture.

We teamed together with the Christian Heritage Church that provided the children with food and games. They had a large number of teachers and other volunteers who fed the children. This made things easier.

In addition to ministering at St. Cyprian's, Mary continued to volunteer in pastoral care for the sick and the dying through a hospice program. She had been doing this ministry consistently for ten years. But as we have mentioned, her challenge came when she suffered from depression. There were several critical incidents that triggered the sickness.

There were rites of passage. After moving from the Episcopal Church we were affiliated with the Diocese of Thika, which was under the oversight of my brother, Bishop Gideon. We had a blessing from Bishop Gideon coming all the way from Kenya to confirm our members. After being with Gideon, we felt the need of having a bishop in America. And so eventually St. Cyprian's, AMIA, and the Thika Diocese entered into a covenant that we will have oversight from an AMIA bishop, but remain affiliated to the Thika Diocese. We had this relationship until I was consecrated a bishop by Archbishop Hartley of Anglican Church Worldwide. These passages were critical to Mary, and as Van Gennep rightly observed, the rites of passage are accompanied with crisis. Every move was reminding Mary of other moves and the crises that accompanied them.

At this time our only son was experiencing conflicts related to adolescence. The incident that made Mary sink into depression was a call we received while we were watching a movie at a theater. We had forgotten to turn off our cell phone. The call came from the police station.

We left immediately and went to the station. Let now Mary speak for herself: "My heart sank when I saw our son drugged with his friend. I never dreamed that our child would do those things after all the instruction and training we have given him." Mary was more hurt by what she saw than our son was. She has high blood pressure and then depression. While she was still taking antidepressant pills, we got a call that my mother-in-law had died. Our financial condition did not allow us to go together. She had to fly alone to Kenya for the funeral. Being the most respected member in the family, Mary had to choose a casket. After the funeral she chaired the family meeting, which decided the individual shares of the family properties. This meeting drained her mentally. As if that were not enough, when she was scheduled to return to the United States, my mother died in her arms as she was trying to resuscitate her.

The death of two mothers whom we loved, and who loved us and prayed for us without ceasing, had a devastating effect on Mary. She had to reschedule her itinerary to attend the funeral of my mother. The week she had planned to depart, our beloved niece, who read a lesson at my mother-in-law's funeral, died. When Mary called and informed me about our niece, I advised her to "Let the dead bury their own dead," and not change her itinerary. I prayed that the Lord would watch over her as she was flying back to the United States. I was overjoyed when I saw her at the Amarillo International Airport. We praised the Lord for protecting her all the way. She was, however, too ill to resume her work at a retirement home. She had to continue taking antidepressants that according to her doctor she will need for the rest of her life.

One of the problems I faced was that I needed to be with her most of the time to protect her from herself and her teenage son, and to see that she took her medicine. But to my utter surprise, even when she was sick, she never ceased serving the Master at St. Cyprian's and giving pastoral care to the sick and the dying.

When I was consecrated bishop, we started with the discipline of having a daily devotion before dawn. We started by singing at least three songs. Then we read the Daily Office, which included four readings, two from the Old Testament, including a Psalm, while the New Testament included the Gospel and an Epistle. We then prayed for all nations, family, and friends. As we continued this spiritual exercise, Mary started recovering and depended less and less on medicine. When she visited her doctor, she was told that she was totally healed and that she didn't need medicine any more. She joyfully is now ministering as the mother of All Nations Christian Church International and has more than one million children. Locally, she ministers to the Sudanese women and ministers in the free youth camp for low income children, gives pastoral care to the hospice patients, and volunteers as a greeter in "Texas," an open air drama in Palo Duro Canyon. Mary's favorite scripture is Psalm 27:

The Lord is my light and my salvation
Whom shall I fear?
The Lord is the stronghold of my life
Of whom shall I be afraid?
For in the day of trouble
He will keep me safe in his dwelling,
He will hide me in the shelter of his tabernacle
And set me high upon the rock.

Her favorite song that she sings every morning in Swahili is:

Sun of my soul, Thou Savior dear,
It is not night if thou be near
Oh, may no earth-born cloud arise
To hide Thee from Thy servant's eyes!

Among the many things that Mary and I have in common is obedience to our Heavenly Father. Material gain has never been a motive behind our ministry. We reach out to whomever God commands us to reach out to. Even though I became patriarch of All Nations Christian Church International and chancellor of ANCCI University, we still minister to "the little ones." In the Philippines we minister to the children of God at the dumpsite. In addition, I minister with and to the archbishops, bishops, and the faculty of ANCCI University. In addition I have a heavy schedule of curriculum development. I still visit refugee families and their children. In spite of her heavy load as first lady of ANCCI, Mary works in the free youth camp and routinely visits the sick and the dying through the hospice program.

CHAPTER TWENTY-SIX:
A TYPICAL DAY

March 11, 2009
The Rev. Mary Githiga

As usual we woke up before dawn for our devotion, which included a balanced spiritual diet. For our wake up coffee we sang three songs, one of which must be "OPEN MY EYES THAT I MAY SEE WONDERFUL THINGS IN YOUR LAW." Psalm119:18. This was followed by the main course, which must include four readings, two from the Old Testament and two from the New Testament. Two of the reading must come from Psalms and the Gospel. We read with a highlighter. The key words for the day were "Do you want to get well? Get up, pick up your mat and walk." John 5:1-18. "Then I will give you shepherds after my own heart, who will lead you with knowledge and understanding." Jeremiah 3:1-18. "It is good for me to be afflicted so that I might understand your decrees." Psalm119:71. "I am not ashamed of the Gospel, because it is the power of God for the salvation of everyone who believes." Romans 1:16.

Since my husband and I minister on a tent-making basis, as did Paul, I had to do the work I enjoy at Canyon Junior High. I love being with the kids. My supervisor seems to like what I do. After work, with tired legs, I drove to the retirement home, where I used to work, for doughnuts for Sunday refreshments and for feeding children during our pastoral visits. The residents love my presence immensely. One lady, who still remembered me by name, told me that she misses me and that she was delighted at my visit. This time they packed enough doughnuts to feed twenty people.

After this I headed to a nursing home where I volunteer for hospice spiritual care. Like I enjoy the school, I also take pleasure in giving pastoral care to three residents under hospice care. I started with a lady who was suffering from Alzheimer's. I was amazed to note that the Spirit had prepared her for spiritual care. She recognized me. I called her by name and she responded. After comforting her with the word of God, we prayed for her. When I finished, she responded with "amen." I left her praising God for the divine communication that had taken place between us.

The second patient was a retired military man. He started complaining, "I had a long day today since they don't allow me to smoke." I told him that smoking was not good for him and that if he allowed Christ in his life, this will satisfy him and he would not have cravings for smoking. "I have told God to get out of my way," he responded.

"God is Almighty and all powerful, and it is impossible to get him out of your way," I retorted.

I also talked to him about the love of God. We then held hands for prayer. As we were praying, I felt God's power transforming the professed atheist. There was a great peace in both of us. Now, instead of telling Jesus to get out of his way, he is letting let Him in, to be his way and truth and life.

The third patient was a retired female judge. This time I found her playing bingo with other residents. The judge introduced me to her friends. They stopped playing bingo to listen to the words of comfort. I reminded them of the presence of the loving Father who is always with us. After we prayed together, they also seemed to have peace and I left them rejoicing.

I then went home. After relaxing my tired legs, I called my husband to check where he was. I learned that he was having pastoral visits. Let us hear what he said about his day.

John

WEDNESDAY IS DEVOTED TO THE children's ministry and working on "the tent" for our living expenses. I am also totally committed to be led by the Holy Spirit. In a night vision, I saw a priest, who lives about 700 miles from us, in anguish. So the first duty was to call him and find out what was going on. His daughter answered the phone. The priest came to the phone and told me that he has been sick for a week. After a word of comfort and encouragement we prayed together. After this I worked on the seminary curriculum development and then checked our rental properties.

Later I visited a Sudanese family on Tuesday. The mother of this lovely family was on Prime News and in the newspaper. It was reported that a thirty-one-year-old woman was charged with arson for allegedly setting clothing on fire the day before at the elementary school. She was charged with a first degree felony that carries a penalty of five to 99 years, or life, in prison. I was deeply grieved with this news, since I knew her and have paid pastoral visits to the family. Her husband told me that she was suffering from acute depression and had refused to go to the hospital. So, moved with compassion, I decided to visit the family. I knocked at the door but nobody answered. Then I called out to them. The nine-year-old daughter answered the phone and opened the door. She was apprehensive and scared. Her younger brothers were crying. The father had gone for groceries, and the daughter now plays the role of mother. After comforting her and her brothers, I left to make a second visit.

As I drove I had a call. This came from eleven-year-old Muhammad. He wanted to know whether I would take them to the children's program today. I told him to remind the other children. In the meantime, I drove to see another Sudanese family. A five-year-old who was crying answered the door.

There was turmoil in the house. A fourteen-year-old was fighting with her young uncle. I separated them and stopped the fight. After calming them, I headed to a Burundi family's home.

Here a seventeen-year-old girl was taking care of her younger brother and sisters. There was peace in this family and all the children came to me. A six-year-old girl wanted to sit on my lap while I was holding her three-year-old brother. I taught them a Swahili chorus. After the song I gave their big sister $5 to buy bread for the children.

After this I went home and found Mary lying on the bed relaxing after a long day. She appeared to be very peaceful with a feeling of accomplishment. She then gave me the highlight of her day and we had supper.

After supper I made a call to one of our priests who is facing foreclosure and is planning to be relocated. I was surprised by his faith and confidence in the Lord. After praying with him, I called one of our bishops to find out how he and his wife were doing. They are both taking Anthropological Approach to Pastoral Care. So we discussed their assignments. They are both great students and great ministers of the Gospel. Our discussion ended at 10:00 p.m. I was ready to retire to bed. As I slept, I meditated on the key words from our morning devotion:

Then I will give you shepherds after my own heart,
Who will lead you with knowledge and understanding.
JEREMIAH 3:1-8

I am not ashamed of the Gospel, because it is the power of God
For the salvation of everyone who believes.
ROMANS 1:16

Shepherding entails taking care of the sheep and lambs, and leading them to green pastures. Guided by the Great Shepherd we take care of children, youths, and adults.

CHAPTER TWENTY-SEVEN:
DOCTORS AND PREADOLESCENTS

Wednesday, October 26, 2007

I don't always understand God's direction as he holds my hand and guides me through the barren land. As His tool, He uses me in whichever way He deems right.

The Being of Light came in a dream to give me a hint of what I have to do. Last night in the dream I saw a medical doctor who was very tall in a black suit and white shirt. There were many people of all ages and races. As we were moving to the meeting place, he decided to return to his car and removed his jacket. When he came back we proceeded to the meeting. He wanted to go through a pile of mud, but I guided him to the right path. Then I woke up and couldn't figure out the meaning of the dream.

My "to do" list included communicating with the dean of the seminary and with seven doctors of theology who are being considered as candidates for faculty positions. I wrote to five of the doctors on the list. For those who are new friends, I sent them a copy of my book *Initiation and Pastoral Psychology*. It was a long and exhausting day. At 3:30 p.m. I took a power nap to have the energy needed for the preadolescents. At 4:30 p.m. I got up and had a cup of tea. I checked with Mary to see if Mohamed had called. He had, but was hesitant to talk to my wife because he was used to hearing my voice. But Mary quickly identified herself and called his name. "Is Father John coming to pick me up for Church?"

"Yes."

"What time?"

"The usual time" Mary responded.

After relaxing I was ready to pick up the little angels. I stopped at Walmart to buy fruit for them to snack on after church.

As I drove, I was contemplating about the children's ministry and particularly Mohamed. I have known him for five years. I used reverse psychology when he was five. I used to pick up his big sisters for the youth program and Mohamed always asked, "Father John, can I come?"

"Not at this time."

When he turned ten I started taking him to the children's program. He was the only child who called to remind me to pick him up. He called me when I was in Phoenix, Arizona, and Jackson, Mississippi. He was the only child who called the other children and reminded them to prepare for church. He refused to be baptized because his dad couldn't permit it. He indeed has the Spirit of Christ.

Arriving at his home, Mohamed was at the door. As we drove he told me that he had already called the other children. We picked up four brothers. As we were going to Joy's house, Mohamed asked, "Father John, When did you become a doctor?" This was a surprise. I didn't know that Mohamed knew that I was a doctor.

"Twenty six years ago."

"How much money do you make as doctor?" asked Wol.

"Being a doctor does not mean making money, it means that you know a lot about something."

"Are you still a doctor?"

"Yes."

And of course I am doctor, doctor, doctor. As we were talking I felt the presence of God. It then dawned on me that God wanted me to be with these little angels to inspire them to greatness. Some of them may become productive members of society and ministers of the Gospel. The Omniscient knows all about it. We arrived at Joy's home. She is twelve and from the Democratic Republic of Congo. To my dismay, we found Joy swimming in her dress in flood waters. When she saw us she hastened to change. Outside there were kittens. All the boys left the van and started to play with them. When Joy came, we all got in the van and within a few minutes we were at the church. They ate all that they could and then played in the gym.

At 7:00 p.m. the kids were in church. As usual the program started in high gear, with boys and girls trying to outshout each other. Then they had to compete in keeping quiet. The program included a girl and a boy giving their testimony about how they prayed and testified at the pole in school. These kids won a few students for Christ. They were applauded and given baskets filled with gifts.

It was now 8:30 p.m. when I was taking the kids back to their homes. I first dropped off Joy, the only girl present, and then the four brothers, and finally Mohamed. They were as prayerful as the wild kittens. I had to ask them to stop playing in the van. But Joy, who was provoking the boys, was almost uncontrollable. When we dropped Joy at home, everybody was calm. After dropping the four brothers off, I was alone with Mohamed. The boy shared with me about another boy who had died. This led to a discussion about life after this death. I asked Mohamed, "Where will you go when you die?"

"I will go to heaven. Tomorrow I will tell everybody about what I have learned in the church."

"Thank you, Mohamed," I responded. "Be strong in the Lord."

After taking Mohamed home I drove to Canyon.

I was home by 9:00 p.m. I was tired but full of joy. I enjoyed some time with Mary, my beloved wife and helpmate. She had prepared a delicacy for me. Thanks be to God for His guidance, love, and care.

I have yet to understand God's plan for the ministry with the doctors of divinity. One of the doctors on my list was going through a tough time. A few days ago we received an email message stating that he was being laid off by the Episcopal Church. He worked tirelessly for the past ten years as the chaplain for three universities. Now he received the results of an evaluation from the mean spirited team who seemed to have become "doctor killers." He was given an F in all areas of his ministry. The fact that he was given the lowest possible grade in all areas certainly suggested that the evaluating team may have had an agenda to push with little regard for the chaplain, the truth, or God's plan for the church.

Fortunately we read the message in the home of Father John and Mother Ruth Urban who had been persecuted by a bishop of the same church. Better still, we were with Bishop Gideon who was a classmate of this doctor in high school and college. As we were discussing the offensive letter, Gideon told us the doctor never got an F in any situation. So we decided to call him, to pray with him, and give him a word of encouragement. We told him he has the three most important "F"s: FAITH, FELLOWSHIP, and FREEDOM.

On Thursday, the Master of the Vineyard directed me to call this doctor, to encourage him and ask him whether he would consider being a potential faculty member of our seminary. In our talk, I told him that what he had gone through, I went through three times. I thought that it couldn't hurt the third time, but it did.

Let me share with you the price I have paid for being a doctor. In all three occasion that I have been laid off, the underplaying issue was jealousy. The ecclesiastical authorities who were supposed to defend their clergy sided with a few lay people, who were gossips or paranoid and spiritually dead. In the last ministry with this church the complaint was that I was splitting time between the University Church and the African refugees and Mexican immigrants.

The second challenge occurred when I was the vicar/chaplain of a predominantly black university. Despite spiritual warfare, the Lord gave us fruitful ministry at the chapel, the university, and in the community. At the chapel we started a weekly Bible study that was attended mainly by the faculty and graduate students. We went through a book of the Bible using discursive methods. Everyone had time to share his/her experiences. We also started a Canterbury program (student/faculty program) that attracted a large number of students. We had a cultural celebration program once a month. Each country represented brought their cuisines, wore their traditional dress, and played their Christian folk songs. Nigerians would dress in their traditional attire and play Nigerian music. It was most interesting to taste a chick prepared by a Jamaican. You would think it was imported from Jamaica. The program attracted many Christians who were not Episcopalians. Being the only chaplain who had a doctorate, a good number of the faculty and mostly the directors and heads of departments came to our office for spiritual direction. I also visited university presidents for encouragement whenever they were under attack. As an adjunct professor of Kiswahili, my class attracted a large number of students. Besides teaching Kiswahili, I taught African philosophy. I really enjoyed being with students. Our class started a Kwanzaa celebration for the university and community. I was always the guest speaker during cultural awareness week. In March 1995, I was awarded a Certificate of Recognition and Appreciation for promoting international awareness and cultural diversity by the Division of Students Affairs at Grambling State University.

But we also had ministry to the children. We started a Press On program for children in the housing project. They are low income families. Dr. Young, a graduate school professor, joined me in visiting the kids and preparing the program for them. Christians from other church families who used to pray with us at the Grambling Christian Center joined the team. In the eyes of the "lay pope," I was becoming too ecumenical.

However, the diocesan bishop, even though he had no doctoral degree, was never jealousy of me. Not only was he pastoral and spiritual, but he was the diocesan spiritual center and spiritual director. His diocesan conventions were both business and spiritual events.

We participated in the planning of the Juneteenth celebration. This commemorates the announcement in 1865 when Texas slaves were told of their emancipation. A ship docked in Galveston, Texas, brought the news.

Our success in the ministry was due to the strong support from my wife, and her gifts of nurturing and hospitality. There were also refreshments for those who attended Bible study. As it was with other women of the church, she had to provide after church breakfast at St. Luke's Chapel. She was also in the altar guild and Stephen Ministry, which visits the sick who are members of St. Luke's Chapel.

Ironically, the more we searched God's will and the more we committed ourselves to the ministry, the greater the warfare. It was very much as when Nehemiah was rebuilding the wall of Jerusalem. He reported, "When Sanballat heard that we were building the wall, he became angry and was incensed. He ridiculed the Jews in the presence of his associate…Those who carried the material did their work with one hand and held the weapon in the other and each of the builders wore a sword at his side as he worked." Nehemiah 4:1-18. Our Sanballat, whom we will call Munjuga, was in the leadership of this congregation for fifteen years and had chased away a number of the priests. Like Doeg, he was a typical priest. On the church committee, he was the only person who had no doctoral degree. He was also a thorn in the flesh to the university leadership. Kicked out of the Baptist Church because of immorality, he joined the Episcopal Church where he was free to do as he pleased, drinking and womanizing. Thus, the more we initiated anything that would uplift the community spiritually, the more I was maligned. He poisoned the granters and, consequently, we lost a third of our stipend. I should admit that the forces of darkness were so agonizing that I developed high blood pressure. My beloved wife became depressed. I still remember an incident when I was going home from a diocesan convention. Weary and mentally drained, I asked God, "God, how long will you let this man sabotage your ministry?" Arriving home, the first call I received informed me that Munjuga was dead. I had to rush to his home to comfort the members of his family. He had, of course, instructed his family that I should not be a celebrant at his funeral. My predecessor, whom he had chased away, was the celebrant. In his homily, the priest talked to Munjuga. "Munjuga, you have contested with powers in the church and at the university. You are now going to face Him who has all powers."

One of the challenges that we faced in the Episcopal Church was that the lay leadership, which had no theology, was more powerful than the bishop. More authority was granted to the more aggressive, the loudest, or materially rich. But this was a refining fire, preparing me for a ministry to those with a jeremiad and the type A folks who are penalized for their achievements. Glory is to God.

Nevertheless, I know of a priest who underwent greater persecution for being a true prophet and being faithful to God. Thus, St. Paul's word is relevant in this regard: "No temptation has seized you except that is common to man. And God is faithful, He will not let you be tempted beyond that you can bear. But when you are tempted He will provide the way out so that you can stand up under it." 1 Corinthians 10:13.

In this regard, I know of a priest who went through a nastier experience. This was an African priest who was called to minister to a black congregation in a certain city in the United States. This priest, who had come from a parish of seven congregations with three thousand members, was surprised to find himself in a small church with empty pews. He, however, enjoyed the hospitality of the African Americans. Being a type A priest, he and his wife exerted all their energy in ministry. Within six months the church was full to the brim. With his wife they started several programs: women's fellowship, men's fellowship, adult choir, junior choir, and the team of evangelists who reached out to the community. Being the most educated priest in the city, he became a priest in the community. He was the most sought after minister during Black History Month. In five years, the priest and his wife had transformed the congregation and the community. He also lectured at the community college. As adjunct faculty he taught nearly every course in the school of humanities.

The challenge started when he published a book that grew from his sermons. He joyfully, but naively, gave a copy of his book to a diocesan bishop during a clergy conference. Astonishingly, the face of the bishop turned red. His comment was shocking. "So you spend all of your time writing books rather than doing the ministry."

After this incident, the bishop believed every rumor circulated by unconverted members of the congregation about the priest. All those who were spiritual pleaded for the priest, whom they dearly loved. But the shepherd of the shepherds sided with the limping sheep and resolved to fire the priest. In their last meeting, the bishop, who had a heavy Southern accent, used two words to summarize the reason why the priest had to go: "Accent and African-ness." Before they left the office the preacher's wife put her hands on the bishop's shoulders, looked at him, and asked, "Bishop, let me ask you a question." The bishop nodded. "Are you a Christian?"

"Yes" answered the Bishop.

"If you are a Christian," the preacher's wife's responded, "you should be listening to good people, not bad people. It can be cold there. Be taking care of your priests."

With these words they parted from the bishop who offered no prayer or blessing, even though they had faithfully ministered in the diocese for five years. For those five years they fought for canonical residence without success. And for that reason, at the Diocesan Convention the priest and I had a voice, but no vote.

Interestingly, on their last day of service, the priest was filled with joy and prayed, "Lord, forgive them." And thus the departure was like a wedding day. The words of our Lord became more vivid than ever: "Oh blessed are you when men revile you and persecute you and utter all kinds of evil against you falsely on my account. Rejoice and be glad, for your reward is great in heaven, for so did men persecute the prophets who were before you." Matthew 5:11.

Having been the only black priest in this diocese, one could easily blame racism for what the priest experienced. But I went through a nastier experience in Kenya from a Kenyan bishop. This is what happened.

I was the only Kenyan clergy with a doctoral degree in the Anglican Church of Kenya. Additionally, I was a professor, the head of the department of pastoral theology, and the Anglican representative at the prestigious St. Paul's United Theological College, with canonical residence in the Diocese of Nakuru. I started ministering in this diocese when I was eighteen. I did house to house and street to street evangelism long before I had any training. I taught religion at the Nakuru Youth Center, where I was training as a painter. For five years I evangelized juvenile delinquents and founded St. Nicholas Children's Home. Ecumenically, I was known for being involved in ecumenical activities. We planted St. Nicholas Church and started the First Nakuru Company of Boys and

Girls Brigade before moving to the United States for higher theological studies. At that time I was two captains in one, Church Army Captain and the captain of the First Nakuru Company of the Boys Brigade. This first company eventually gave birth to numerous companies all over the country that are run by Presbyterian, Methodist, and Anglican churches.

Nevertheless, I returned from the United States to educate the shepherds and to safeguard the interest of the Anglican community. I was also appointed by the archbishop of Kenya as provincial correspondent. The position entailed being a go-between with the Anglican Church of Kenya and the Anglican Communion. One of my functions at the time included representing the ACK to the Afro/Anglican Conference, which was held in Barbados, West Indies.

In addition, I became founder-president of the African Association for Pastoral Study and Counseling, a continental body which brought pastors, pastoral counselors, and psychologists together. Years later this association held its first congress on African Pastoral Studies in Kinshasa, Democratic Republic of Congo.

Now was a golden opportunity to attend my first diocesan synod. I had to go a day before to visit with my spiritual father. Immediately after arriving in the city, I called the bishop for an appointment. With a very dark voice he asked, "Did you bring your surplice and cassock."

"No," I responded. He then hung up on me.

My spiritual father had to sacrifice great things for small things. I had to see him the next day at the synod. He started the deliberation with roll call. Everybody, including his European guests, were called. My name was not called. I then stood and asked why my name was omitted. The response was annoying. "We are going to treat you as a visitor with no voice and no vote." Dismayed, I left the synod and went to the Nakuru Game Park, a place I used to go for prayer and meditation when I was ministering juvenile delinquents. I had a great time with flamingos, cheetahs, deer, and waterbucks. I found joy with the game and Mother Nature. Nevertheless, I should also admit that I couldn't sleep that night. Being stressed, I coughed the whole night. I, however, lamented with the psalmist:

Save me O God!
And the flood sweeps over me.
For the water has come up to my neck
I am weary with my crying;
I sink in the deep mire,
My throat is parched
Where there is no foothold;
My eyes grow dim
I have come into deep waters,
With waiting for my God.

After the dark night of the soul, the Lord stood by me and encouraged me.

While I was assured that the God of all comfort was with me, I had to cry again with the psalmist:

Hear my cry, O God;
Listen to my prayer.
From the end of the earth I call to you;
I call as my heart grows faint;
Lead thou me to the rock that is higher than I.
For you have been my refuge,
A strong tower against the foe.
I long to dwell in your tent forever.
And take refuge in the shelter of your wing.
Psalm 61:1-4

These words brought healing and forgiveness. I spent the remaining days in Nakuru visiting friends and spiritual partners. I learned later that the bishop was suffering from an inferiority complex. He was reported to have said that I was looking down upon him from the peak of Mount Kenya. He perceived himself at the bottom while I was at the top of Mount Kenya. The underlying issue was fear and jealousy. These were the same attitudes I found with the American bishops. For instance, I learned from close friends of the bishop who fired an African bishop for his accent and African-ness, that he would have done the same to an American priest who demonstrated to him surpassing gifts of teaching, preaching, or writing.

This episode, being as afflicting as it was, was for my own good and for the good of my future ministry. This is so, since this bishop was not only a member of my ethnic group, but was also very supportive of me in the morning of his life and my earlier ministry. He was also a model priest. In the twilight of his life he became paranoid. He used clergy transfers as whips. A priest could be ordered to move to another parish within twenty-four hours. This is why we have to take the words of St. Paul seriously: "Have this mind among yourselves, which is yours in Christ Jesus." When he was on the cross, with excruciating pain, his words were "Father forgive them, for they know not what they do." I could also add, "Father forgive them, for they are mental patients." Many a servant of God has suffered terribly, not so much because of demonic activities, but from mentally ill church leaders, who may be either bishops or lay popes. This is a call for wisdom for the body of Christ.

Mombasa Episodes

One more episode, which was more amusing than painful, happened in 1983 when I was attending the Consultation of Anglican Theologians in Mombasa, Kenya. I was conversing with Archbishop Gitari when two police officers alighted from their jeep with handcuffs in their hands and asked, "Where is Dr. Githiga?"

Archbishop Gitari who knew exactly what they were looking for responded, "This is Dr. Githiga, but he is not a medical doctor." At this time, medical doctors had gone on strike for pay raises. It was illegal for medical doctors who were employed by the government to strike, and they were being arrested.

This episode brought a flashback of several uplifting and educational incidents which occurred a decade before in Mombasa, which were very much like Mombasa mythologies. We used to hear there were jinni in this town (Muslim spirits). You would see a black cat that could convert to a jinni and start talking to you.

While I never saw a jinni, it was in this town that I got parish experience when I was a student at St. Paul's United Theologian College in the early 1970s under Provost Givan who was a European missionary. I had a lovely time with this celibate priest. We agreed on many things, but also disagreed on a few things. The Provost believed in being positive at all times, and that could mean not reading any negative Psalms. He informed me that if I selected a negative Psalm for our morning prayer, he would not respond to it. The sermon should not exceed nine minutes. I argued, "You cannot worship God with an eye on the clock." So when my turn came, he reminded me while we were vesting that if I exceeded nine minutes, he would leave me alone.

The sermon took thirteen minutes, but by the time I finished, my mentor had left. When we met at home, I asked him where he had gone. His response was humorous. "I went to pick up my girlfriend at the railway station but she was not there." We laughed. Besides teaching me some British ways of life, the provost guided me to the power of positive thinking. I learned that hasira hasara. Anger is a loss.

When I was still with Canon Givan, I had another humiliating incident that occurred when I was attending a show for President Kenyatta. This was a night when the president was being entertained by traditional dancers. Being a proud theological student, I looked for the best spot closest to the president. I walked there majestically, as Kenyatta advised us several times during his public rally. After taking a seat, a suspicious plainclothes police officer came up to me and asked, "Who are you?"

"I am a theological student," I responded proudly.

"What is Geleological?" the man asked angrily. Before I had time to define the word theology as the queen of sciences, he said, "I am asking, who are you in the government?"

I told him I was not a government official. He commanded me to move away from my seat. I then stood in the crowd where I was pressed by the plainclothes policewomen who were checking whether I might have a weapon. At this time I remember the words of our Lord: "He who exalts himself will be humbled, and who humbles himself will be exalted." I also recalled his advice to the disciples that when they are invited, they should not take the best seat.

Interestingly, for a long time I thought that I was the only one who was embarrassed trying to be closer to a Kenyan president. But I discovered others had a worse experience than I did. I discovered this when my wife and I were invited to dinner by the Rev. Dr. Cyprian Kimathi, who was my student when I was teaching at St. Paul's United Theological College, and his wife. Just for laughs, I shared my Mombasa experience. Habel Gitogo, my nephew, and Helen Kimathi amused us also. Habel was with an athletic team that had visited President Moi. His coach greeted President Moi by genuflecting, holding his right palm with his left hand and stretching his hands to shake the president's hand. Before he had touched him, two bodyguards grabbed him, and by holding the skin of his right and left ribs, raised him in midair. The third guard struck the back of his head. The innocent young man suffered great pain. Helen Kimathi was on the team that had entertained the president. As she moved closer to the president, she was pressed by other students and touched the president's vehicle. The innocent teenager was caned. This recalled the Holy Scripture: "No temptation has overtaken you except such as is common to man, but God is faithful who will not allow you to be tempted above what you are able, but with a temptation will also make a way to escape, that you may be able bear it." I Corinthian 10:13. So whatever you are going through, realize that others have gone through it, and possibly more painfully than you. This sharing gave me profound love for my Master, who is the King of Kings. Not only can I be close to the Lord of all that is, seen and unseen, but I can also be in Him.

Listen to what he says. "Here I am! I stand at the door and knock. If anyone hears my voice and opens the door, I will come in and eat with him, and he with me." Revelation 3:20.

For fifty-two years I have been dining with Him. If you don't have this relationship with Him, call on Him. You will be surprised to discover that He is as close to you as your nose is as close to your mouth. Unlike political presidents, the King of Kings will be with you forever. More importantly, He will make your life productive. He puts it this way: "I am the vine, you are the branches, if a man remains in me and I in him, he will bear much fruit; apart from me you can do nothing." John 15:5.

Why don't you call upon Him using the song below?

Jesus my Lord, my God, my all,
Hear me, blessed Savior, when I call.
Hear me, and from thy dwelling place

Pour down the riches of thy grace.
Jesus my Lord, I thee adore
Oh, make me love thee more and more.

When Christ comes in, praise Him with this song:

Jesus, my Shepherd, Brother, Friend,
My prophet, Priest and King,
My Lord, my Life, my Way, my end,
Accept the praise I bring.

The incident with the police and the president's bodyguards gave me a flashback to my first visit to Mombasa. This took place in the mid-sixties when I was ministering in Nakuru. The journey to Mombasa was a highlight of my life. I was attending the National Christian Council of Kenya Annual Youth Consultation. The event was like a well-deserved vacation since I was living a very busy life.

I was a captain of a newly founded Company of Boys' Brigade. The program was run jointly by the Anglican and Presbyterian churches and met weekly to build up children and youth. I was also fishing the troubled kids from the streets and the dumpsite. I was the organizing secretary of the NCCK Youth Department, Nakuru branch. Our program included monthly interdenominational youth services that brought together choirs from nearly all Protestant churches, ranging from Anglicans to the Salvation Army.

Commitments to the community plugged me into seventeen different committees so a trip to Mombasa was an energizing event. The journey took one and a half days. For the first time, we got to travel in the first class section of the train, the place that just a few years before was reserved for Europeans and Indians. We had a bed in the compartment. As we were going to bed, my friend jokingly bid me good night by saying, "Good night, Captain White."

"Good night, Captain Brown," I retorted.

During the consultation that took place in the Kanamai Youth Center, we enjoyed each other as we shared our experiences in youth ministries. I learned how to swim in the vast waters of the Indian Ocean. The ocean demonstrated the greatness of the Creator and the relaxation reminded us of Paul's words: "For by grace are you saved through faith; and that is not of yourselves, it is a gift of God: Not of works, lest any man should boast." Ephesians 2:8-9. Additionally, the ocean reminded me of a Negro spiritual:

Oh! Stand the storm, it won't be long,
We'll anchor by and by,
Stand the storm, it won't be long,
We will anchor by and by.

My fourth visit to Mombasa occurred in 1998 when I took a group of twelve missioners to primarily strengthen the shepherds and their spouses. After being afflicted by Judas and Doeg, the priest killer, I had now developed compassion for the priests and their families. I knew firsthand what it meant to wrestle with this demonic spirit. I was invited by Bishop Okiring, my seminary mate, and by Bishop Kewasisi and Bishop Kalu, both my seminary students. After holding the retreat in Katakwa and Kitale Diocese, we were now heading to Mombasa, about 500 miles away. We drove a van. I was taking Doyle and Caroline Volentine, Mary, and our son Isaac. The journey from Nairobi to Mombasa was most challenging, full of potholes. Doyle had lots of pain as he had to sit on a boil on the bumpiest road. One of the miracles was that we didn't have a flat tire. The other miracle was ministering to the sixty-five clergy and spouses who now had my students as their chief shepherds. To fuel my joy, the Very Rev. James Mlamba, the provost of Mombasa Cathedral, was my student. Being with him brought interesting memories of St. Paul's. James was a saintly student who visited the faculty and their families to give them pastoral care. We remembered the fellowship where he was assigned to give his testimony. He stood up, turned the pages of his Bible, and said, "I have lost the paper on which I had written my testimony." Everybody burst into laughter, since we all expected his testimony to come from his heart rather than from a piece of paper. In this retreat we had Ramtu, who was a classmate. He expressed his gratitude. This was the very first retreat for the clergy and their wives.

Besides comforting and encouraging the shepherds, the Lord performed signs and wonders through the Volentines. A young couple who had been childless asked the Volentines to pray for them that they might have a baby. Three months later, the Volentines received a letter informing them that the wife was pregnant. Glory is to God. I still cherish my Mombasa experiences.

My fifth experience in Mombasa was an overwhelming reward and far beyond my expectations. This took place November 9-18, 2011. I took three American missioners with me to minister at a Crusade and Clergy Leadership Conference that was organized by All Nations Christian Church International, of which I am a patriarch. As Archbishop Metropolitan Doyle Volentine, the Rev. Bill McMahan, the Rev. George Bates, and I flew to Mombasa, we were assured of our safety by God's word:

I lift up my eyes to the hills,
Where does my help come from?
My help comes from the Lord,
The maker of heaven and earth.
He Lord will keep you from all harm.

Psalm 121

The Lord indeed kept us from all harm. The other words that were very encouraging were:

> *The Lord is my light and my salvation;*
> *Whom shall I fear?*
> *The Lord is the stronghold of my life;*
> *Of whom shall I be afraid?*
> Psalm 27

Surely, the Lord protected us and gave us traveling grace.

Archbishop Kombo did a superb job in planning and scheduling. We started with the Gospel Crusade. The music was of the highest quality. The singers danced to the glory of God and were joined by the congregation. Evangelist Joel Njoroge and Dr. John Kombo (both Kenyans) preached the first day. Their ministry included healing and deliverance. The following day Archbishop Doyle and I ministered the Word. We indeed felt the presence of God. The third day we had the Rev. George Bates assisted by Rev. Bill. Their message was powerful and anointed, and was followed by deliverance and healing.

A large number attended the leadership conference, which lasted three days. Rev. George, using the parable of the Good Samaritan, emphasized the importance of the three keys to fruitful ministry: character, courage, and compassion. These virtues are fundamental for spiritual leadership. Bill, using his experience as a pilot, described how God could locate where we were like a GPS. His message was well received. Bishop Doyle spoke on the Holy Spirit, the fruits and work of the Holy Spirit. In addition, the Spirit used him in prophesying to the participants. I spoke of an anthropological approach to pastoral care, emphasizing pastoral care to the parishioners as they go through the passages of life.

On Sunday we preached in various churches. Archbishop John Thon and I ministered at Christ Temple Community Church, which was planted and is ministered by the Rev. Collins and Mrs. Milford. They focused on holistic ministry, the spiritual, physical, social, and economic needs of the parishioner. The service was very spirited with great music and friendly Christians.

For our relaxation we participated in a safari to the Shimba Hills National Reserve, which is famous for African elephants. Although the elephants were hiding that day, we enjoyed seeing other animals: giraffe, waterbucks, monkeys, and buffaloes. We also enjoyed lunch there.

The crowning joy, however, was the presence of three bishops and three archbishops: Archbishop John Thon of All Nations Anglican Church in Southern Sudan, The Most Rev. Elias John Kombo, archbishop of All Nations Province of Equatorial Africa, The Most Rev. Doyle Volentine, archbishop metropolitan, The Rt. Rev. James Mararo, the Rt. Rev. Maurine Shali, and Rt. Rev. David Ngure. I had overwhelming joy for these Shepherds of the Shepherds who are members of ANCCI. I was humbled by the fact that God used our hands to enthrone the three archbishops and to confer a Doctor of Divinity on two of them. This reminded me that when I was a boy, one of my greatest passions was to see a bishop. My father, being a lay reader in our local church, promised me that when the bishop visited our church he would put me on his shoulders so that I might see the bishop. My father went to glory before we had an episcopal visit. A bishop's visitation was very rare because there was only one bishop whose jurisdiction included the whole of East Africa: Kenya, Uganda, Tanganyika, and Zanzibar. So it was a real blessing to minister with these bishops and archbishops in Mombasa.

On November 17 we left for the United Kingdom. We were delighted to meet with Bishop-elect Steven at London City Airport. He took us to a Holiday Inn where we stayed for four days. Our activities included touring London, and visiting with Bishop Michael and Dr. Ruth Reid. We prayed with Ruth who was battling cancer. We praised God for her faithful ministry. On Saturday we visited Apostle Williams' new facility, which is big enough to be a cathedral All Nations Anglican Church. We praised God for this precious gift. Apostle Williams then hosted us at a Chinese restaurant where we had a fruitful fellowship. On Sunday we worshipped in Christ Faith Tabernacle, which is under the oversight of Apostle Williams. Each of us had time to give a brief message. We were indeed edified by the sermon of Apostle Williams and by the music of the Spirit-filled congregation. Following worship, CFT hosted us for dinner. This was highlighted by golden time with the first lady, the Rev. Oma Williams.

On November 21, 2011, we left for the United States praising God for his provision and protection. Reflecting on our mission, I perceived phenomena that might have a prophetic message. Our journey from Mombasa to London was extremely foggy. Because of this, the flights from Nairobi to Amsterdam and from Amsterdam to London were delayed. Our journey from London to Amarillo, Texas, was the same. The clouds and fog seemed to symbolize the day of the Lord, which is very much like a woman in labor pain.

The global village is going through pain caused by economic crisis and Muslim extremists. The major newspapers reported daily the war between Al-Shabaab and the Kenyan armed forces, *linda Inch* (defend the homeland). The East African nations and the African Union are teaming together to fight the common enemy. This satanic force is anti-Christian, anti-western civilization, and against all non-Muslims. We are witnessing horrors that preceded the day of the Lord. According to the prophet Joel: "The sun will be turned to darkness and the moon to blood before the coming of the great and dreadful day of the Lord." Joel 2:11. Our Lord predicted: "Nation will rise against nation, and kingdom against kingdom there will be earthquakes in various places and famines…Brother will betray brother to death and a father, his child. Children will rebel against their parents and have them put to death." Mark 13:8, 12-14. Is this not happening in our time? Consider Vladimir Putin, the Russian president causing upheaval in Ukraine and provoking the European Union and the United States by telling them that Russia is a nuclear superpower. Think about the totality of evil with ISIS and Boko Haram. ISIS is giving Christians four choices: convert to Islam, pay heavy taxes to Islamic governments, flee, or die. These children of God have opted to flee and are fleeing to rocky mountains with nothing. Boko Haram is just as evil. Think about how they kidnapped Nigerian students from the examination room. These girls were aspiring to be doctors, engineers, teachers, and businesswomen. Now they are reduced to nothing, are forced to be Muslims, and are sold as slaves. As if that is not evil enough, they are being trained and forced to kill their relatives, including their parents. We are indeed seeing the abomination that causes desolation standing where it does not belong.

With regard to the economy, there is a yawning gap between rich and poor. So many people are hurting in the global village, including in the United States. So many people are jobless and homeless and hungry. I believe these upheavals are ushering in the coming of the Lord. We have to bear in mind that He who came is simultaneously coming, and He will finally come at the end of time. He is the one who was, who is, and who is to come. The phenomena we have mentioned, I believe, is ushering in a great revival. This is very much in keeping with Joel's prophecy: "And (after the day of the Lord) I will pour out my Spirit on all people. Your sons and daughters will prophesy, your old men will dream dreams, your young men will see visions. Even on my servants, both men and women will I pour out my spirit in those days. I will show wonders in heavens and on earth, blood and fire and billows of smoke."

Both in Mombasa and the United Kingdom we saw these manifestations of the Holy Spirit.

The day of the Lord has a message for you and me. We have to watch and pray. When Jesus predicted His coming in Mark 13 he concluded: "What I say to you, I say to everyone: 'Watch.'" Apostle Peter tells us in a nutshell what we must do while we await the coming of the Lord: "For this very reason make every effort to add to your faith, goodness; and to goodness, knowledge; and to knowledge self-control; and to self-control perseverance; and to perseverance godliness, and to godliness brotherly kindness, and to brotherly kindness, love. For if you possess these qualities in increasing measure, they will keep you from being ineffective and unproductive in your knowledge of our Lord Jesus Christ." II Peter 1:5-8.

I still believe that all of the great and challenging moments, which we mentioned earlier, were vital preparation for the ministry to All Nations. The God of all knowledge and wisdom was in control and had our best interest at heart. He also had the best interest of all those who will come to our path.

As I'm writing this chapter, there is a knock at the door. It is 8:00 p.m. Opening the door, it was Dr. Strong For Ever (the meaning of his name). He is from Taiwan. I have been his mentor for seven years. He normally comes to me at night and when there is something that is bothering him.

His face looked pale, his eyes were drained. Mary asked him whether he needed some food. "No," he responded.

"How about something to drink?"

"I would appreciate that," he replied.

Mary gave him a glass of passion fruit juice. As he sipped the juice he started pouring out his problems. He had just come from an interview for an open position in mechanical engineering. He was one of the two finalists. He was not selected. This was one of the many interviews he has had since he got his PhD. His work permit and student visa are expiring. He now has to register in a community college to maintain his status. He is also hunting for a job. He has two things against him: being a foreigner and having a speech impediment. The present hurt is reminding him of the many hurts he has shared with me for the last seven years. This includes rejection by two supervisors who happen to be Taiwanese professors. One of them insulted him verbally. "Your mother gave birth to a fool." His girlfriend deserted him. He was emotionally wounded by his father when he was not doing well in high school and undergraduate school. So the father, an atheist, has willed his real estate to Strong For Ever's sister. For that reason he has no desire to go back to Taiwan. His suffering is much greater than mine.

Our friend went on sharing until 1:00 a.m. I reminded him of the very meaning of his name "strong forever" and God's precious promise: "I will lead the blind in the way that they know not. In the path that they have not known I will guide them. I will turn the darkness before them into light, the rough places into the level ground. These are the things that I will do, and I will not forsake them." We advised him to forgive and to resist doing anything destructive. We then finished up with prayer, A few days later I received a thank note from Strong For Ever:

Bishop John:

> *I would love to thank you for your warm encouragement in my harsh time this year, and your messages you sent to me every week really give me hope to face the challenges in my life.*

> *Sincerely yours,*
> *Debby.*

The more we reached out to the people of all social strata and all nations, the more the Loving Father opened the door for mission and gave us a clear vision.

CHAPTER TWENTY-EIGHT:
A CLEAR VISION

MAY 28 - JUNE 25, 2010

THE LORD GAVE US A clear vision as we set out for our mission to Kenya. We were to lead a retreat for pastors and to consecrate the shepherds of the flocks. The Lord assured us that He is our Great Shepherd and will provide for us, using us to empower the shepherds whom He had prepared before the creation to lead His sheep. The guiding scriptures came from Ezekiel 34:11-15. God promised: "I myself will search for my sheep and seek them out...I will feed them in good pastures." As with David, we were assured that "The Lord is my Shepherd." God also promised: "And I will raise up for myself a faithful priest, who shall do according to what is in my heart and my mind, and I will build him a sure house, and he shall go in and out before my anointed forever." The Lord fulfilled these promises far beyond our expectations. All the events were like a divine carnival. We were fed spiritually even before delivering the message.

At Liana High School, we experienced God's mighty presence as 1200 young men were singing and dancing in the Lord. We were awed by the ministry of Chaplain Edward Etale, our seminary student. Rev. Mary and I gave the message to a very attentive audience. We sang for them "The Lord is My Shepherd" in Swahili. After the service we enjoyed hospitality from Chaplain Etale and then joined Bishop Ruth and Lisa Wong at the ordination of Martha Muzungu. This event was marked with joy. Martha and her congregation were very much like the name of their ministry, Joy Land Ministries. A delicious lunch included cutting ordination cake, which Rev. Martha fed the congregation as the bride would feed the bridegroom. I have never seen anything like it!

The retreat for pastors followed. The topics that were covered included fruitfulness in ministry, divine healing, and knowing your rights in Christ. There were praises and worship. The event concluded with a healing service conducted by Bishop Ruth and Archbishop Elias John. Most of the pastors were bi-vocational. The majority of them were teachers. Following the retreat, Bishop Ruth and I taught seminary students. Bishop Ruth lectured on Spiritual Formation, while I taught anthropological approaches to pastoral care. The students were eager and interactive.

The retreat was followed by the consecration of bishops George Musandile and Stanly Karanja. George and his wife, Jenny oversee Four Fold Church in Zambia; while Stanley and Margret oversee the Kingdom Builders Network that concentrates on reaching out to the teachers and the head students. We were very much impressed by the spirituality of these bishops and their wives. They are indeed a great gift to the church.

The next day we had the enthronement and consecration of the Archbishop Elias John Combo. The event was a musical festival! The service, which was held at the University of Nairobi, attracted a large crowd. Elias was consecrated as archbishop of the Vision Evangelic Ministries and All Nations Province of Equatorial Africa. He brought to All Nations gifts of healing. He preaches the Gospel with manifestations of signs and wonders, particularly in healing and deliverance. He has planted churches in all seven provinces of Kenya and has a ministry in Norway.

On Monday, Archbishop Kombo took the mission team to the Nairobi National Park. We enjoyed seeing all kinds of animals. The most impressive were a lion and lioness, who comfortably lay in the middle of the road as though they were posing for a camera. We drove closer and closer to them, but they refused to move from the road and expected us to drive on the roadside. As we watched them lying fearlessly, they reminded us of the Lion of Judah, and that with Jesus (the Lion of Judah) we can smile at the storm. They reminded me several times that I heard Jesus say, "It is I. Do not be afraid."

On Tuesday, Archbishop Kombo took us to Masai Land. We were given a hero's welcome by the Masai who slaughtered a goat for us. Symbolically, this was an act of giving the very self. We enjoyed delicacies before the service. We were culturally and spiritually enriched by the Masai with their traditional clothing and African Christian folk songs. When preaching, we were affirmed by hand clapping. We left Masai Land rejoicing in the Lord who bonded us with the Masai. On the way to Nairobi, we had a flat tire in a small village. As we were working on the vehicle, two Kikuyu young men came and told us that they wanted to commit themselves to God. Mary and I delightfully led them to Christ.

On Wednesday, Archbishop Kombo took us to Ichichi, the place where I was born. The road was bumpy and hilly. We were totally surprised by the Holy Spirit in this church that is pastored by my nephew,

Stephen Mbatia. We were given a warm welcome by the congregation that included my brother, sisters, and old friends. Bishop Ruth and Lisa were well received. There was heavy anointing and divine healing as Archbishop Kombo made an altar call. I have never seen this happen at Ichichi. To crown it all, the archbishop asked worshipers to come and shake my hand. Each person shook my hand and gave shillings that amounted to 750 Kenya shillings, which was a lot of money for an Ichichian. We felt loved, affirmed, and energized.

On Friday, June 11, we drove to Nakuru, Mary's birthplace. Saturday we ministered to the Congregation of Yahweh, which is under the oversight of Pastor Susan, the wife of the Rev. John Mwaniki. We were once again awed by the Holy Spirit in the way the congregation (which was all Kikuyu, my community) worshiped in the Spirit and in Truth, and at the same time claimed our Jewish heritage. They preferred to address God as Yahweh and Jesus as Yoshua. Interestingly, there is a parallel between Jewish and Kikuyu heritages. For both, the fig tree is a national symbol. The meaning of the name Kikuyu is "the people of the fig tree." For both, circumcision is the means of becoming a full member of the community.

On the afternoon of the same day, we went to Kiti to minister with the Sudanese under the oversight of Archbishop John Thon. We were given a cordial welcome. The Lost Boys, who were clad in white shirts and black pants, performed Christian dances with a lot of skill and prepared the congregation for the message. Bishop Ruth had the message of encouragement for women, which was well received. After the service, we were served Sudanese traditional cuisine.

On Sunday, Bishop Ruth and I went to St. Nicholas Church, which I planted thirty-six years ago. This church birthed several parishes. It holds three services in English, Swahili, and Sudanese. The church is at St. Nicholas Children's Home, which I started 44 years ago. This church is my joy and my crown. We had arrived on Saturday to inform the vicar that we were in the city and would like to give a message. Before the service commenced, however, Bishop Ruth and I were called to the vestry and informed that we could not preach, but only greet people and sit in the congregation. We were invited to speak during the announcements. Ruth spoke for three minutes. When I stood, I spoke briefly for three minutes about how we started. During the fourth minute I was served with a note that said "time to stop." I then quickly remembered Paul's words: "Woe unto me if I do not preach the Gospel."

So, I quickly told the innocent audience about the secret of a fruitful ministry, which is recorded in John 15:5. Our Master says, "I am the vine you are the branches. He who abides in me and me in him, he it is that bears much fruit, for apart from me you can do nothing." The incident also reminded me of the words of the Apostle John: "He came to that which was his own but his own did not receive him. Yet to all who received him, to them who believed in his name, he gave them right to became the children of God." John 1:11. We learned that the very meaning of being a bearer of Christ is rejection and reception.

After this Bishop Ruth and Lisa Wong departed for Nairobi while Mary and I were left visiting with families and friends. On the same day, we worshiped in Nakuru Cathedral where I was ordained a deacon and priest. Here we were well received and were given a chance to give a report about our ministry. We had a blessed meeting with the bishop of Nakuru and his wife, old friends, and members of our family. The whole service, which included a wedding, was uplifting.

Interestingly, although prevented from ministering at St. Nicholas, the following day, boys who had lived in the St. Nicholas Children's Home, found their way to a home where we were visiting. These lovely children of God are musicians who call themselves the "St. Nicholas Harmonies." They sang for us and expressed their appreciation. "We are most grateful you started St. Nicholas," said one of the boys. "If it were not for you, we couldn't be what we are." These fruitful children have produced a CD entitled "Jesus is the Answer." They eagerly listened to the story of how we started the home in 1966 and the church in 1974. They enjoyed immensely spending time with their "spiritual grandparents."

We spent our last week in Kenya visiting with families in Nakuru, Nairobi, and Ichichi. The word that the Lord gave us during our fellowship with the families was from Proverbs 17:17: "A friend loves at all times, and a brother is born for adversary." We praised our Heavenly Father for giving us brothers and sisters who are both friends and prayer partners. We also praised God for all our Christian friends who prayed for us and gave financial support to the ministry. The more you prayed for us and gave us financial support, the more the Lord used us as spearheads.

May God bless you and supply your needs according to His riches in glory.

CHAPTER TWENTY-NINE:
MISSION TO SUDAN

December 24, 2013, found me at the lowest ebb and I was crying with the psalmist: "Oh my soul why are you downcast?" I was constantly listening and reading news about the newest nation of Southern Sudan. Looking at my 2009 diary, I learned that on December 24, 2009, I was in Duk, Jonglei State, which was having crises. I remembered how in 2008 God revealed to me in a dream the challenges that we had to face. The dream also predicted the current crises.

In the dream I saw myself with one of our Anglo bishops. As we were following our guide, my fellow bishop became sick and I had to walk holding his hand. Our guide, who was tall, walked faster without looking behind. As we were climbing the hill, the guide disappeared on the other side of the hill.

As we walked with the bishop who was so spirited, but with physical weakness, the road forked. We didn't know which path to take. When we were in Bor, I saw the landscape that I had seen in the dream. Our fifteen days in Southern Sudan were characterized by exaltation and humiliation, opportunities and crises. Our schedule included visiting with then Vice President Salva Kirr and the governor of Jonglei stat. We watched the enthronement of Archbishop John and two other bishops, conducted open air preaching, saw the consecration of St. Paul's cathedral, and attended a clergy conference.

We flew from Nairobi to Juba on December 19 on a JetLink jumbo jet, and on the 20th we ministered the church in Juba. We went without breakfast, hoping for breakfast in the church. The service was spirited and went from 11:00 a.m. to 4:00 p.m. After the ministry of the word, women brought water in a basin, pulled off our shoes and socks, and washed our feet and hands. It was a challenge for them to put the socks back on wet feet. But we felt greatly honored.

At 5:00 p.m., hungry and exhausted, we were led to a restaurant for dinner. We were accompanied by seven men. Each of them placed an order, but little did we know that we had to pay for everybody.

On the 23rd we chartered a plane from Juba to Duk. While this sounds great, we had not budgeted to rent an aircraft. However, we had the joy of having the archbishop, his family, and the diocesan staff with us. Landing at Duk, we were given a hero's welcome. We were led to the convention by the musical band. We felt loved and appreciated. I asked Bishop Doyle to be the first preacher.

When he stood, he said, "I am not accustomed to this heat." As soon as he said that, he suffered heat stroke. Here the road forked, since I didn't know whether to take care of the bishop or continue from where he had stopped. The challenge was even greater since there was no hospital, no telephone network, and the plane had left.

The Bishop was escorted to a small hut where he was given first aid by a deacon and two ladies. They were wetting his head and fanning him with a handkerchief. On one hand I had to deliver the word to a large multitude, and on the other I was concerned about what was happening to my companion. After the service, I went to the hut and found that my brother had recovered, even though he was still weak.

I was led to a tiny hut next to that of my friend. This was to be my lodging. It looked like a Masai hut. To enter one had to crawl. The door was not secured and anybody could enter.

Inside, the hut was too hot for my friend and so he had to sleep outside. The deacon slept next to him to take care of him. I slept inside where I was visited by lizards and crickets.

We were guarded by fifty young men, who slept outside the cathedral compound that adjoined our huts. They were noisy, however, because everybody tried to outshout the other. It sounded like the voice of many waters. This continued until 2:00 a.m.

On the 24th we had an enthronement service for Archbishop John and two other bishops that was attended by 2000 congregants. On Christmas day we had an open air service. Those in attendance included chiefs and the congressmen.

Six parishioners spoke before we preached. They told us about their afflictions. Two of them narrated how an Episcopal bishop had them arrested because they had become Anglicans.

On the 26th we had a clergy conference. Just as I started talking, Archbishop John told me that they had a gift for me and I needed to go and see it. It was a horned bull. I was told to touch it and pose for a photo. "It is not going to hurt you," said John. "It is yours to take with you to the United States." I told them to slaughter the animal for the clergy.

Immediately after this great honor the road forked. Going back to the class, I found my companion, who could barely stand because of his physical weakness, sidetracked by the clergy. They asked for clerical shirts, and they needed them here and now. Our guide had informed them that we would provide them with clerical shirts. The bishop told them that we brought only our own shirts. I had to take them back to class. We tried to engage them by using the Bible discussion method, but we learned that the majority of them couldn't read.

After the session we were visited by the women delegates, dressed as our mothers used to dress fifty years ago. Their leader started with a question. "What made you consider visiting this place?"

"Why?" I asked.

"Because this is a place where after God created the world, He forgot all about this place," she replied. "Look at us. None of us has ever gone to school. Besides we travel a very long way to fetch water."

These mothers requested two things: a girls' school and a well. Eventually, I learned that Dinka women are the most valuable and least educated. To get a wife, a young man has to give between fifty to a hundred head of cattle.

On Sunday we had a service with 1500 in attendance. The service started at 7:30 a.m. We were astonished to see that everybody had to bring their own chair. I saw children bringing cans that they used as a seat. We experienced the presence of God. Archbishop John spoke on stewardship, while Bishop Doyle and I preached the Gospel.

After the service the road forked again. Our guide told me that he expected us to provide the bishops with return tickets. Our funds were now depleted, but I gave each of the bishops $20. One bishop said, "This is not enough. I borrowed money to come here and if I don't pay back the lender, I will be arrested." We were made to feel guilty for sins we had not committed.

The night before our departure for Bor I had a nightmare. I saw a tall man forcing himself into my unsecured hut. When I woke up, I found that it was not a dream. There was a tall man standing in the room. He said, "You must provide the bishops with the money for their return tickets and you also have to fuel the governor's vehicle."

Learning that this was my guide, I told him, "Don't talk to me about money again!"

"You are my father," he responded. "And I must talk to you as a son." He then left, but I couldn't sleep again.

In the morning the lovely mothers prepared chicken for our last breakfast. When my companion smelled the aroma, he could not even taste it. We encouraged him to eat, but he couldn't. "I know John will buy me some fruits on the way." So after fueling the governor's van we started our journey to Bor. On the way we saw hundreds of head of cattle. But there wasn't a grocery or restaurants. My companion became sicker. He was vomiting constantly, but he had an empty stomach. This was bad for type 1 diabetics who are supposed to have at least four small meals a day. We arrived in Bor at night. We were housed with an Anglican lady, but she didn't have any food. So we headed to town. As we were passing through a homestead, a group of short people stopped us.

A short young woman started beating our vehicle with a large stake as she talked loudly and angrily. Our driver, who was much taller and stronger, got a hold of her and grabbed the stake and threw it away. He then jumped in the van, reversed, and took a different route. He turned off the light and we had to depend on the moonlight. Driving through the bush, I feared that we would have a flat tire or fall in a ditch. As we drove, I asked the driver what the short people were saying. "Get away!" he said. "You have come to grab our land." By the time we arrived in town we had a flat tire. We changed it and then looked for a restaurant. There was only one. My companion asked me to bring him ice cream and canned beans. However, the only food that was available was roasted beef (nyama choma). The smell of nyama choma was offensive to my companion and he could not put it in his mouth. I was now concerned since he had spent the whole day with an empty stomach. Now he had to sleep on an empty stomach.

Worse still, in the morning of our last day there was no breakfast. The water for our shower was a handful of water that the hostess poured into the palm of our hands. We then had to go to Bor to board the plane.

While we were purchasing the tickets to Juba, the agents found that the dollar notes were older than 2005. He then took the liberty of reducing a dollar to 60 cents. We were left with $125, of which a $100 bill was unacceptable either in Sudan or Kenya since it was a 1999 bill. We flew to Juba, which I renamed Juba-poverty for the experience we had to face. We arrived at 9:00 a.m., an hour before the departure of the JetLink jumbo jet. The agent at the ticket counter told us that she didn't see our tickets in her computer, and that she required $600 for our tickets to Nairobi. As we were negotiating, the plane left. We were now two bishops in the airport who were very hungry, impoverished, and exhausted. While we were praying for divine intervention, the airport manager called the agent and us to his office. Looking the agent in the eye he asked, "Do you want to tell me that these two men of God are lying? And that you are right and they are wrong?"

"It is not me, it is their agent. We don't find their tickets in our computer."

The confrontation was effective. The agent told us to follow her downtown to the JetLink office. We had to hire a taxi and follow her. We had only 200 Sudanese pounds and $125. The miracle occurred at the downtown office. We called our travel agent in Los Angeles, California, and she spoke to the JetLink agent and our problem was solved. However, being New Year's Eve, there were no flights on New Year's Day so we had to stay in Juba one more day. We asked our taxi driver to take us to the United Citizen Lodge where our guide was. As we arrived we told him that we were short of funds. "You are men of God," he responded. "Just give me what you can." We gave him 100 Sudanese pounds. This was angelic. We were delighted to see Archbishop John. I told him that he had to find us some money for an exit visa in Nairobi. The following day he gave us $50. The providers had become beggars. We were indeed married to Lady Poverty.

In the morning of New Year's Day we walked to Matumish Hotel, which was owned by a Briton who is married to a Kenyan. It was a half a mile walk. I held the hand of my companion as we walked as he was too weak to walk alone. When we arrived there, we enjoyed air-conditioning and watched CNN. We ordered breakfast, but were doubtful we had enough money to pay for it. Graciously, 100 pounds was enough. We stayed there for three hours, enjoying an environment that was closer to our own.

We didn't have money for two days' stay in United Citizen. We asked our guide to take care of it. He was now drinking from his own cup.

On January 2, 2010, we were in Juba airport. We now had $50 for an exit visa in Nairobi. But little did we know that we had to pay $75 for the airport tax. Now the poor bishops learned to bargain.

I told the officer that we had only $50. By another miracle, he said, "It is okay." We boarded the plane. I sat next to a Sudanese American who was heading to the United States. We visited and he became a friend. He was another angel. I told him I had a $100 bill that would not be accepted in Jomo Kenyatta International Airport for an exit visa and that if he had newer dollars, I would trade him my 1999 bill for $50. My new friend joyfully accepted the deal.

After landing we walked slowly to customs. My companion had to sit several times. After getting the exit visa for $50 (this was all the money we had) we headed to baggage claim. I was overwhelmed with joy when I saw the driver of Bishop Gideon, my brother. We had no money for taxis, but now we had an angel driving us to the bishop's home. Thus ended our ordeal. Bishop Doyle received money from Rev. Carolyn and I had some money in Kenya. So we both said goodbye to Lady Poverty, hoping she will not seduce us again. We stayed with Bishop Gideon's family for three days and recuperated. Then on January 6, 2010, we flew to the United States and on the 7th at 7:30 am we arrived in Houston. I was overwhelmed with joy when I saw Carolyn. She was another angel. I handed Bishop Doyle over to her safe and sound.

We can say that in all the things we went through, God was in control and had our best interest at heart. By being in Sudan for sixteen days, we developed an empathic understanding not only for the Sudanese, but also for the people of God who had undergone such tribulation. Better still, the Lord strengthened the bond between Archbishop Doyle and me. For sixteen days, we had no mirror (something we take for granted) and so we were mirrors for each other. We, indeed, owned a great promise, "You shall receive power when the Holy Spirit has come upon you, and you shall be my witnesses…to the end of the age."

Our Master fulfilled his promise. "And surely I am with you always, to the end of the age."

SOUTHERN SUDAN TODAY

As I am writing this message there are terrible massacres in Bor and Jongelei state. It is estimated that 10,000 people are dead and 825,000 have fled to the neighboring state. As Mr. Wai, an eyewitness of the massacre put it, "When I saw the bodies, I broke into tears." He said, "I was devastated. I don't have words to describe it. I was asking 'Why, why, why are they being killed?'" The questions why and what needs to be done, need to be addressed. The major problem is political. The power struggle between Salva Kiir and Dr. Machar. The two are poisoning their ethnic groups against each other. Politics also deals with the issue "Who gets what and how much?" There is an inability to accommodate diversity. Each community has a different language and culture. When diversity is not appreciated, there is a "thou-it" relationship whereby each community perceives the other as an "it." The most important question is, "What must we do to get out of the crisis?" As Pope Francis recommended, "Everyone needs to be a peacemaker." Peace making means talking positively about the other person and the celebration of diversity.

Sudan needs a prophetic voice from Sudanese religious leaders. This prophet should be God's mouthpiece who is fighting for justice without favoring his community, is willing to challenge his own community, and if need be, is ready to die for all communities. When Kenya was struggling with authoritarianism whereby the ruling party was the parliament and judiciary, it was religious leaders who had prophetic messages that dismantled the system. The battle was won when one of the most outspoken bishops was assassinated. His death dismantled authoritarianism and ushered in a multiparty system.

Finally, it can be argued that only the water which flows from the people's desert can survive the heat of their desert. Thus the answer to the problems in Sudan will come from the Sudanese themselves.

Nevertheless, as Christians we are called to stand in the gap for those who are suffering. The Bible admonishes us to bear one another's burdens. I like the way Apostle John puts it: "I, John, your brother share with you in Jesus the suffering and kingdom and patient endurance that is ours in Jesus Christ." Revelation 1:9.

CHAPTER THIRTY
MISSION AND THE CROSS

MARCH 2013

AS DR. MARTIN DAVIS AND I were preparing for our mission to Kenya, I faced something that I had written about, but I don't like experiencing. Pain. A week before we took off I had a toothache. The dentist found I had a crack in my tooth and recommended a root canal. Before I had opened my mouth for the orthodontist, I looked at him and said, "Don't do a root canal if it is not absolutely necessary. If it is a gum problem, just treat the gum!" Surprised at a patient who spoke with authority, he looked at his watch, stared at me, and then told me they were going to take X-rays to make sure I needed the treatment. After taking ten X-rays, he told me that the procedure must be done before I left for mission. After sitting for two hours with my mouth open, I felt as though a big stone was grafted in my jaw. The enemy was laughing at me. "We have zipped his mouth. He will not be able to talk." Yet the Spirit spoke to me using the words of St. Peter: "Casting all your cares upon Him, for he cares for you." To my surprise, by the time we landed at Jomo Kenyatta Airport in a British Air jumbo jet, I had no pain. Gabriel, our tour driver, took us to the ACK guest house. The following day we visited Margret, my sister-in-law, who fed us a delicious lunch.

After lunch we drove to Murang'a. It was delightful to meet Bishop James who led us to the Queen's Hotel where we stayed for two days. All the clergy who attended the conference were Spirit filled, teachable, and loving. Dr. Martin spoke about the Holy Trinity for hours without notes. I spoke about having a fruitful ministry. At the end of the event we had an evaluation and found the following: We had the right audience-church leaders who were teachable with uplifting music, hospitality, and had give-and-take attitudes. They recommended that the next time we needed to talk about Christology. After the conference Bishop William drove us to Ichichi and we spent a night in his home. The next day Canon Habel insisted that we stay in his home. "We need you to stay with us because no Mzungu has ever slept in our home since the foundation of the world." During a family get together, Martin was the focal point of attention and everybody wanted a photo with him. Ichichi Christians were hospitable. Not only did they feed us, but they also took a love offering for us that amounted to 4,600 Kenya shillings. This was the actual cost of our travel expenses from Nairobi to Ichichi.

On our journey to Nakuru we visited St. Paul's University, which was my academic home for eight years (three years as a student and five as faculty). At the gate there were three women guards who had to check our vehicle, and then we visited with Prof. GalGalo, the vice chancellor who took us around. We visited Dr. Esther Mombo, deputy vice chancellor, who was one of my students. She reminded me about the Githiga Foundation Fund, which my brother Gideon and I started to award books to the students who exceled in pastoral theology and missiology, the courses we taught when we were faculty. As we were touring St. Paul's we got a call from Ken Otieno informing us that the pastors were waiting for us. We shortened our tour and headed to Nakuru, the city of my youth and where I was ordained a priest and where Mary was born. As we exited to go to Section 58, we found Ken who guided us to the conference sight. The music and spirit were high. During the morning of this day, I had advised Martin that we dress casually, but put on the cross. I was, however, amazed to find that most of the participants were wearing three-piece suits. Like the shepherds in Murang'a, they were Spirit filled, teachable, and receptive, and with inspiring music. But unlike Murang'a, these pastors came from different church families and different communities. They also requested that we come back.

The following day we toured Nakuru game park where there were thousands of flamingoes. This lake has more flamingoes than any other lake in the world. All the game was well fed and enjoyed posing for a snapshot. From there we visited St. Nicholas' Children's Home, which I founded for juvenile delinquents in 1965. In those days I hunted for children of the dumpsters. They were called children of the dumpsters and whenever children in the neighborhood saw my motorcycle, they sang "mapipa, mapipa" (dumpster). I am so grateful to God because ANCCI is feeding children at the dumpsite in Nakuru and in Iligan City in the Philippines. Now the center has many children, a high school, and the church we planted in 1975. After the visit we went to see Mary's sister, Jane, who entertained us and gave us lunch. We had a great time with the in-laws.

The following day we had to leave for Kisii. As you can see in Dr. Davis's report, the road from Kericho to Kisii was extremely rough and dusty. I felt for Dr. Davis who sat on the front seat, and for whom children were singing Mzungu Mzungu (white man) even when he was trying to take a nap. Through God's protection we arrived at Kisi safely and were taken to the Mash Park Hotel. The following day we journeyed to the conference site. As Fr. Martin wrote, "The road was dusty and hilly, so by the time we reached the audience our black suits were dark brown and our heads covered with dust." The first thing our host did was to dust off our clothes and our heads. Entering the church we found Pastor James Sobora from Tanzania teaching. He appeared to be a good teacher. Then Fr. Martin and I taught until 6:00 p.m. on an empty stomach. By this time I was feeling exhausted and dizzy. Worse still, we had to climb the mountain because we were too heavy for the car. Driving back to the hotel we had a second dosage of dust. Upon our arrival Bishop Thomas gave me a prescription, "Take a liter of hot water." I drank a liter (1/4 gallon) of hot water while Dr. Davis drank a bottle of cold soda. We then appeased our empty stomachs with a chocolate bar. This was dinner for hungry and exhausted doctors. For me, dust and heat result in pneumonia or an asthma attack. Miraculously, I didn't suffer from these conditions. I didn't even use my inhaler. I am grateful to the Great Physician and for answering the prayer, "protect them hali na mali."

The following day, we had to journey to Kisii Mountain. As usual the people of God were full of joy. Better still, Sophia Gwako had instructed the women to prepare lunch for us. On the third day we had Sunday service, which was well attended. A large number of worshippers could not get a seat in the church and so they worshipped outside. Everybody danced in spirit. They all seemed to enjoy God.

We also had the blessing of ordaining three church planters as bishops with apostolic succession. After the service we headed to St. Angela's Orphanage. Astonishingly, when the children saw Dr. Davis, they thought they were seeing a ghost and so they fled for their safety. The only child who had courage was Angela. She was the very first child to be admitted and the orphanage is named after her. We had a good visit with the teachers.

After this we went to the church, which is ministered by Pastor Francis Matoke. We had met Francis on Friday when he showed me the Letter of Affiliation that I had sent him a few days before I left the United States. He was a victim after the election of 2007. He was shot with an arrow and had a scar on his head. His testimony brought tears to my eyes. He said, "I praise God for what they did to me. Before this suffering I didn't know God. But the suffering brought me to Christ. I have forgiven them and I pray for their progress." Francis' church included nine orphans. After the service we had a meal and a lovely discussion in his house.

The Kisii ministry, though most challenging, was also most fruitful. The following day we went to Nairobi and spent the night in the home of Bishop William Githiga. As usual, Helen prepared a delicious meal for us. Her compliment was interesting. She said, "I love you and I appreciate you because the only thing that you could not eat is a piece of metal." Bishop William appreciated me because I was cool, and Martin because he was receptive, patient, and diplomatic.

The following day, William took us to Jomo Kenyatta International Airport where we began a 32 hour journey. Arriving in Amarillo in the evening of the following day, the weather was the opposite of what we had in Kenya. In Kenya it was very hot, and here we had eight inches of snow. Mary was unable to drive into our driveway, so she called Garang, our seminary student, to come for me. He succeeded in driving me home, but as he was driving home, his car slid in a ditch. Being too tired to do anything, I told Garang to take our car and the following day we would get someone to pull his car out of the ditch. The following day I had to call AAA who brought a wrecker. As the wrecker was struggling to pull the car out, it slid into the ditch. The driver tried to pull himself out without success. A four-wheel drive truck came to our aid, but the wheels started spinning. Finally, he was pulled out by a caterpillar tractor. The struggle took three hours. This was the day that I was supposed to sleep for ten hours. Being so tired and disorientated, I went to bed and slept like a dead man. After eight hours of sleep, I saw a little creature walking in the room. "Where am I?" I asked.

"You are in your bed," the creature responded.

"And who are you?"

"You have been away only for two weeks and you cannot remember your wife?" I was so sorry to note that it was my dear wife who I had not recognized.

Once again I had to face something I had written about but I didn't like going through. And that is confusion and temporary disorientation, which we undergo during rites of passage. The challenges were tripled by sleeping in seven beds in seven different bedrooms in three different time zones, and ministering with Christians with a diversity of cultures, plus jetlag. For more information see *Initiation and Pastoral Psychology* in the chapter on Lostness.

We are most grateful for all those who prayed for us and those who gave us financial support. I still remember a prayer of one of our seminary students: "Mungu uwalinde hali na mali" [God protect them in all circumstances (hali) and all that they possess (mali)]. I recited this prayer every morning. And God indeed answered the prayer.

To this end, if God calls you for overseas mission, know that he is able to provide and protect. In the words of our Master: "And whatever you ask in my name, that I will do, that the Father may be glorified in the Son." John 14:13. He also promises: "I will be with you always, even to the end of the age." Matthew 28:2.

CHAPTER THIRTY-ONE: MOTHER'S DAY

MAY 11, 2014

I AM WRITING THIS MESSAGE on the centennial celebration of Mother's Day. The founder of the day was Anna Jarvis who was the tenth child of thirteen siblings. By the time she was born, her mother Anna Reeves Jarvis had lost nine of her children. So Anna knew the deep pain of a mother losing a child. She started her campaign for mothers when her own mother was very sick and living with her and her brother. Anna, who never married or even became a mother herself, became the mother of Mother's Day. Interestingly, Anna was inspired by her Sunday school lesson when she was teaching at St. Andrew's Methodist Episcopal Church. She concluded with a prayer: "I hope and pray that someone, sometime, will found a memorial mother's day commemorating her for the matchless service she renders to humanity in every field of life."

She became the person whom God used. On May 10, 1914, after a tireless campaign, President Woodrow Wilson declared the second Sunday of May a public holiday. Now, this Mother's Day in 2014 has found mothers with unbearable pain for their 230 daughters who were abducted in Nigeria by a terrorist. He claims that god (Satan) has told him to capture the girls and sell them. The main issue sparking their manner of abduction was the education the girls were receiving and that the leader of Boko Haram regards as a sin. The girls were captured when they were sitting for the national exam. The timing was calculated. While this brought fear to mothers and daughters, it also produced female heroes and has inspired girls in Islamic countries to continue to pursue education. Fifty-one Nigerian girls jumped from a running vehicle and fled. Please continue to pray for the abducted innocent girls and their families. Pray for all women in countries where women are dehumanized.

We are also delighted to inform you that the Rev. Dr. Mary Githiga was recently honored for her eleven years of dedicated ministry to hospice patients. The family of a now deceased mother, to whom she ministered, wrote this note to Mary:

Dear Mary,

Thank you for the wonderful care you provided to our mother! She always enjoyed your smile, kind heart, and tenderness. We always knew she was in good hands.

Love,
Deloris

———

Dear Mary

I want to thank you for the special care you gave my mother. You have the special gifts of kindness, patience, and love, and you carry it over in your work. You bring them joy and laughter. Mom enjoyed living at the Hudson, and always looked forward to your smile. Thank you for all you have done.

Mary Hiner

And now to Him who is able to keep you from falling and to present you before his glorious presence without fault and with great joy—to the only God our Savior be glory, majesty, power, and authority, through Jesus Christ our Lord, before all ages now and forevermore! Amen

CHAPTER THIRTY-TWO:
JULY IS A MEMORIAL MONTH

JULY 2012

THE MOST COMMEMORATIVE MONTH IN the United States is July with the Fourth of July holiday, also called Independence Day. On July 4, 1776, the Declaration of Independence was adopted and America declared its independence from Great Britain. Independence Day is commonly associated with barbecues, carnivals, picnics, concerts, fireworks, and parades. Surprisingly, this month is the most memorable for me, and the All Nations Christian Church International. I was born on July 7, 1942, and born again on July 13, 1958. ANCCI was incorporated in Texas on July 27, 2007, and on the same day we were granted 501 C 3 status by the federal government as a not-for-profit ministry. Remembering my birth motivates me to ask for a birthday gift. I would like to share the desire of my heart by sharing the message of a dream I had when I was in Phoenix, Arizona. After ordaining Dr. Elizabeth to the diaconate, my mother-in-law, Joyce, appeared in my dream wearing a dress with bright colors and a white handbag. She appeared beautiful and in good spirits. "I have to take you home," I told her.

"Not at this time. I don't deserve you. I need to be educated first and then I will come."

To get the message in this dream, you need to know about my relationship with my mother-in- law and the unique contribution

Arizona has made to our ministry. Joyce was so loving and always on my side. Mary told me how her mother confronted her for missing our date when we were courting. My mother-in-law prayed for our ministry and us until she was called to glory at 96 years old.

Arizona is a special state for me. It was there that I paid my first Episcopal visit. It was there that I received the first two ANCCI bishops and held the first House of Bishops. I was enthroned archbishop on an Indian reservation in Arizona. Our website was built and is being mastered there. Three of the chartered members of ANCCI are in Arizona.

The images in the dream symbolize the desire of my heart. I yearn that all our ministers may be fully equipped for ministry by taking advantage of our University.

Our ultimate goal is to offer theological education to all our ministers so that we may give answers to those who ask us about our faith and may teach true doctrine. We aim at "perfecting of the saints, for the work of the ministry, for edifying of the body of Christ…so that we are not tossed to and fro, and carried about with every wind of doctrine." Ephesians 4:12-14.

CHAPTER THIRTY-THREE: CHRISTMAS MESSAGE

December 2013

Dear Friends,

Grace and peace from God our Father and our Lord Jesus Christ.

I am writing this message with overwhelming joy flowing from the Spirit of Him who became what we were, so as to make us what He is. "The Word became flesh [all that is human except sin] and dwelt among us full of grace and truth; we have beheld his glory, glory as of the only Son from the Father." Becoming what He is. This is the process that starts from conversion and continues until we are called to glory and when He will come again. We experience inexpressible joy when we celebrate Christmas in Christ. Listen to what the Angel said: "Be not afraid, for behold, I bring to you good news of great joy which will come to all people. For to you is born this day in the city of David a Savior, who is Christ the Lord." The more we exalt God in Christmas the more we experience the joy of the Lord. I like the way John the Baptist answered his disciples who complained that "all [John's followers] were going to Jesus." The Baptist responded, "Therefore this joy of mine is now full, He must increase, but I must decrease."

To fuel the joy of Christmas, we must refrain from materialism and unrealistic expectations. We need to pray constantly in the Spirit and remain plugged into the Spirit. Connect your mind and soul with things that build you up spiritually. Turn to religious channels on TV and radio, be a part of a fellowship group that meets on a weekly basis, attend church regularly, and reach out to other people. Use the three keys to success: FORGIVING, GIVING, and THANKSGIVING. We are sanctified by the inspiration of the Holy Spirit, and by keeping our spirits, souls, and bodies sound and blameless at the coming of the Lord. In Paul's words, "Rejoice in the Lord always and again I say, rejoice." The joy of the Lord is our strength. Let us pray that the Lord fills us with peace, love, and joy in the New Year.

CHAPTER THIRTY-FOUR
57TH SPIRITUAL BIRTHDAY

Praise the Lord! Today, July 13, is my 57th spiritual birthday. And as the loving Lord called John and James on the same day, He saved my elder brother, Habel, and me on the same night. We have experienced inexpressible joy of the Holy Spirit. The Spirit of Christ has brought so many people to Christ through us. Sing with us the song of praise below. If you have not committed yourself to Christ do it as you read this message. He is as close to you as your nose is as close to your mouth. This is what He says, "Here I am! I stand at the door and knock. If anyone hears my voice and opens the door, I will come in and eat with him and he with me." Revelation 3:20. When he becomes your friend He will give you very precious fruits which are: "love, joy, peace, patience, kindness, goodness, faithfulness, gentleness and self-control." Galatians 5:22. If you have committed yourself to Christ, be assured that He is able to save and keep you. Listen to what He says. "All those that the Father gives me, nothing can snatch them from my hand." So if He has kept my brother and me for fifty-seven years, He will keep you as well. When He comes into your heart, He gives you eternal life. This is what he says, "I have come that they may have life, and have it to the full." John 10:10. When you get this life, not only are you blessed, but you also become a blessing. Here is what He said to the Samaritan woman, "Whoever drinks the water I give will never thirst. Indeed, the water I give him will become in him a spring of water welling up to eternal life." John 4:14.

1 Come, let us sing for joy to the LORD; let us shout aloud to the Rock of our salvation.

2 Let us come before him with thanksgiving and extol him with music and song.

3 For the LORD is the great God, the great King above all gods.

4 In his hand are the depths of the earth, and the mountain peaks belong to him.

5 The sea is his, for he made it, and his hands formed the dry land.

6 Come, let us bow down in worship, and let us kneel before the LORD our Maker;

7 For he is our God and we are the people of his pasture, the flock under his care.

8 Today, if you hear his voice, do not harden your hearts.

Interestingly, my official apostolic succession scripture is John 13 since there are twelve patriarchs before me named John. The list includes St. John Chrysostom who prayed: "Almighty God, you have given us grace at this time with one accord to make our common supplication to you; and you have promised through your well-beloved Son that when two or three are gathered together in his Name you will be in the midst of them: Fulfill now, O Lord, our desires and petitions as may be best for us; granting us in this world knowledge of your truth."

Being patriarch of All Nations Christian Church and Ministries, which is an association of churches and ministries in over seventy countries with a membership of over two million, I constantly pray for wisdom for shepherding the people of God who have diverse cultures.

CHAPTER THIRTY-FIVE: NEW YEAR'S MESSAGE

January 2014

Solomon said to the Lord, "Therefore give to your servant an understanding heart to judge your people that I may discern between good and evil." 1 Kings 3:9.

Interestingly, Solomon did not ask for wealth or power to dictate to those he governed, or to destroy his enemies. Rather, he prayed for wisdom so that he may distinguish between right and wrong.

This is the best prayer for the New Year. We need to pray for wisdom from above. As the Apostle James puts it, "…the wisdom that comes from heaven is first of all pure, then peace-loving, gentle, willing to yield, full of mercy and good fruits, impartial and sincere." This wisdom is fruitful. Those who possess this wisdom are peacemakers. They sow in peace and raise a harvest of righteousness. James 4:17-18.

Those who lack this wisdom are partisans with dead faith. They have form but no substance. They are dry wells with untamed tongues, and impatient, earthly, and unspiritual. The Apostle Paul would define those without wisdom as those who dwell in their sinful nature. "The acts of the sinful nature are obvious: sexual immorality, impurity and debauchery; idolatry (worship of self, money and power) and witchcraft; hatred, discord, jealousy, fits and rage, selfish ambition, dissensions, factions and envy, drunkenness, orgies and the like." Paul concluded that "those who live like this will not inherit the Kingdom of God." We could add that they are not in the Kingdom of God, FOR THE KINGDOM OF GOD IS WHERE GOD'S WILL IS BEING DONE.

When we submit ourselves to God and repent of our sins, the word of God has good news for us: "If we confess our sins, He is faithful and just and will forgive us our sins and purify us from all unrighteousness." 1 John 1:9. When this precious work is done, we become like wise virgins who had oil in their lamps. We automatically attain wisdom from above. We bear the fruits of the Spirit, which are love, joy, peace, patience, kindness, goodness, faithfulness, gentleness, and self-control.

When we live with and in the Holy Spirit, the reward is great both in this world and in the world to come. Jesus put it this way: "I am the vine, you are the branches. If a man remains in me and me in him, he bears much fruit; for without me you can do nothing." John 15:5.

Our prayer for you is that you be filled with wisdom from above, that you may bear the fruits of the Spirit. We pray that you will submit your time, talent, and treasure to God that at the end of all things the Master will say to you: "Well done, good and faithful servant! You have been faithful with few things, I will put you in charge of many things. Come and share your master's happiness!" Matthew 25:21.

The Lord bless you and keep you;
The Lord make his face shine upon you
And be gracious to you;
The Lord turn his face toward you
and give you peace.
Numbers 6:24-26

When the Lord blesses us we become a blessing to all the people of God, to our families, and to our spouses.

CHAPTER THIRTY-SIX:
A HUMAN BEING IS HUMAN BEINGS

(Mtu ni watu)

ONE DAY I WAS HOLDING a conversation with a man in his 70s as we walked in a mall. "Do you have a family?" I asked.

"No. I live alone, but I do have a girlfriend. We have been friends for twenty-seven years."

"You have been together for twenty-seven years and have never thought about marriage?"

"Well," he responded, "I was married for twenty nine years. Then we divorced. I don't want to go through divorce again. And I am afraid if we get married she will ask for a divorce."

Many, like this man, have partners who live with them but fear to marry because they are scared of divorce.

In Jesus' time divorce was so prevalent that women feared to marry. This was due to a wife being treated as a thing. She had no legal rights whatsoever. She could be divorced against her will. She could be divorced because of adultery or indecency. Indecency included putting too much salt in food, walking with a strange man, or if the husband found a woman who was more beautiful than her. The school of Rabbi Hillel puts it this way, "If a wife cooks her husband's food, over-salting it or over- roasting it, she is to be put away."

Note the Pharisee's question, "Is it lawful for a man to divorce his wife?" He did not ask, "Is it lawful for a woman to divorce her husband?" Our Lord Jesus Christ answered the question with a question. "What did Moses command you?" They told Jesus that Moses allowed a man to write a certificate of divorce, and to put her away. Jesus told them, "For the hardness of your heart he wrote this command- ment." This might have meant that Moses laid it down because it was the best he could expect from his contemporaries, who were still in their infancy in interpersonal relationships. Their anima was underdeveloped. Or it may have meant that Moses was trying to control a situation that was degenerating. He was not really giving permission to divorce. To correct this, our Lord set up a high and holy standard for the principles of marriage. He refers to the original institution of marriage in creation as the union of one man and one woman. "A man shall leave his father and mother and be united to his wife and the two will become one flesh." As the Wisdom of God, the Lord added, "What God has put together let no man put asunder."

In all healthy marriages, the husband and wife relationship is unique. It is amazing how the two become one flesh. Having been married to my wife for thirty-eight years, we relate to each other in a special way. Her joy is my joy, her pain is my pain. She is the very first person I look at in the morning and the last person I see at night. She calls to me more than anybody else.

Marriage is indeed the most important institution for both the husband and wife, and the family. As the Book of Common Prayer puts it, "The union of husband and wife in heart, body and mind is intended by God for their mutual joy; for their help and comfort given one another in prosperity and adversity, and when it is God's will, for the procreation of children and their nurture in the knowledge and love of the Lord." So the marriage partners are advised "not to enter into it unadvisedly or lightly, but reverently, deliberately, and in accordance with the purposes for which it was instituted by God."

Anglican Bishop Ryle advises, "Happy are those who in the matters of marriage observe three rules: the first is to marry only in the Lord, and after prayer for God's approval and blessing. The second rule is not to expect too much from their partners, and to remember that marriage is, after all, the union of two sinners and not of two angels. The third is to strive first and foremost for one another's sanctification. The more holy married people are, the happier they are. Christ loved the church, and gave himself up for her, to make her holy."

The lessons are a profound teaching about what it means to be a human being. They teach that a human being was created as a social being, who can only lead a healthy life by being in a group. Remember! The Lord said, "It is not good for a man to be alone." Interestingly, humans were created by God in his plurality, while everything else was created through the word with a formula: "And God said...and it was." God, however, used a different formula for human creation. He said, "Let us make man in our own image; after our own likeness and let them have dominion." Then God created them male and female. So we are created for God and for each other. Thus, you have to remember that you were created for others and cannot be an island unto yourself. This being the case, we have to constantly fight the demon which disrupts our fellowship with one another. We must conquer a judgmental spirit which produces "a better than thou" attitude. We have to be aware of the fact that humanity is nurtured and revitalized by other human beings. As Waswahili puts it, "Mtu ni watu." A human being is human beings.

Our Lord Jesus is also teaching us that marriage is for life. This is a Christian ideal. This should be a secret ambition of every Christian youth. I admired one youth group member from the Democratic Republic of Congo. As we were discussing future goals, she said, "I will marry a man who is Christian, who can respect and love me and my family, and who has long term goals. I also would like to be a perfect mother." My comment was, "That is a good goal. Do not forget that we are not perfect. But you have to envision the ideal." I should admit that before I proposed to my wife I had observed her for nine years in youth fellowship, youth camp, church choirs, Sunday School teaching, and as an officer of the Girls' Brigade.

I also visited her parents and observed how she related to them. She was also doing the same to me. And interestingly, the good qualitis that I observed has not changed.

It should be mentioned that when the ideal is not attained, there is forgiveness. The Apostle Paul reminds us that by grace you have been saved through faith; and this is not your own doing, it is a gift of God, not because of works, lest any man should boast. Ephesians 2:8, 9

In addition, a healthy marriage includes leaving and cleaving. The married partners must leave their parents graciously and cleave to each other. They should not allow in-laws or former girlfriends and boyfriends to interfere with their relationship. What God has joined together let no man put asunder.

In conclusion, whether married or not, we need to remember that we were created as "us" for "us" to become "we." We should wage war with the spirit of individualism, which is producing narcissism. We have many humans with extreme self-love. We are challenged to count others better than ourselves. We need to ask ourselves the question that Rabbi Hillel posed to himself: "

If I am only for myself, what am I? And if not now, when?"

The above philosophical statement challenges us to be a part of the community. As Professor John Mbuti summarizes the African ontology "I am because we are, and since we are, therefore, I am," as a Swahili proverb puts it, "Union is strength." (Umoja ni nguvu.) We become victors when we face the challenges together in the power of the Lord of Hosts.

CHAPTER THIRTY-SEVEN: BE STRONG, FEAR NOT! BEHOLD YOUR GOD

I STILL HAVE VIVID MEMORIES of the events of September 11, 2001. I remember fear within and without, which characterized the collective and personal life. On this day a police officer knocked at our door with the information that our church treasurer was involved in an accident and was in a critical care unit in the hospital. Rushing there I found that he had been declared clinically dead. After administering the unction, he came back to life but with some brain damage. I was faced with many questions as we also watched the horrible news of massive destruction. Who will take his place? Who will pay the bills? Who will take care of his two thousand head of cattle? At the same time I was preparing talks for a cursillo weekend since I was the spiritual director for the event that was to start on September 13. We didn't know whether the candidates would show up. Being in campus ministry, we gathered together the students for prayer on the campus. More than two hundred students attended the prayer around the flagpole in the rain.

Other people were experiencing greater agony than I was. Some had lost their loved ones. A spouse, a husband, a parent, a colleague, or a friend.

On that day of intense suffering God used many angels to demonstrate his might and power. Not all angels were human. There was an angel dog that saved more than nine hundred people at the Twin Towers. The human angels included Tom Burnett, a pilot who was a passenger on Flight 93. He called his wife Deena to let her know what was going on and what they were planning to do. Tom and some of the other passengers overpowered the hijackers and averted the aircraft from possibly crashing into the White House. They sacrificed their lives for their country. According to Deena, Tom's heroic act drew upon his strong character, which he had developed from his long relationship with God. He had a habit of attending Mass every day. He drew his strength from the God of all power and might. These selfless people and a dog might have heard the voice of the Creator:

Be strong, fear not, and behold your God. Be strong, fear not, behold your God is our theme.

We have to be strong and act in spite of fear because of Who God is.

Our God is a God who is coming.

Our God is a God who is coming with vengeance.

Our God is a God who is coming with a reward.

Our God is a God who opens the eyes of the blind

Our God is a God who opens the ears of the deaf.

Our God is a God who makes the tongues of the dumb sing for joy.

Our God is a God who brings springs of water in the desert.

Our God is a God who brings hope to the hopeless.

Our God is a God who makes the new heaven and the new earth.

Our God is a God who keeps his promises.

Our God is a God who gives justice to the oppressed.

Our God is a God who sets the prisoners free.

Our God is a God who lifts up those who are bowed down.

Our God is a God who cares for the stranger.

Our God is a God who sustains the prisoners.

Our God is a God who reigns forever.

Our God is a God who gives every perfect gift.

Our God is a God who is calling us to be his mouth and his feet.

Our God is a God who is calling us to reach out to our neighbors.

Let us not wait until there is a 9/11 in our lives to act.

We are being called to let God be God of our lives.

We are being reminded we have to trust and obey God.

Trust and obey, for there is no other way to be happy in Jesus,

But to trust and obey.

When we trust in the Lord and abide in Him, we become the channel of the living water that flows to all people, including atheists.

CHAPTER THIRTY-EIGHT:
VICTORY OVER DEATH

OCTOBER 2013

Death, where is your victory?
Death, where is your pain?

These words have comforted me while mourning the deaths of the innocent killed by jihadists at Westgate Mall in Nairobi, and the Christians who were killed at All Saints Church in Peshawar City, Pakistan, by the same evil spirit. I shopped at Westgate Mall in February 2012. So I know very well this magnificent building where you can get almost any item that you are looking for. When I was there, I was looking for a briefcase with four wheels. Some years back you could not get this item in Kenya. There were so many people shopping. The mall is not much different from Westgate Mall in Amarillo, Texas, where my wife and I go to shop and relax. What brought a lot of tears was that these innocent people were murdered by Al-Shabaab in the name of Allah. They targeted Kenyans, Americans, and non-Muslims. It was painful to see the photos of the innocent shoppers who were murdered. They included women and children, and the majority of them were Kenyans. There were also Canadians, Italians, and French victims.

While I was still weeping for the saints who had lost their lives in Kenya, I received an email and photos from our evangelist in Pakistan reporting that 150 people were killed at All Saints Church on Sunday. Another 130 were injured and the victims included women and children. We were directly affected since we have eight ministries in Pakistan, which included two children's Bible schools and a seminary.

We have a ministry that empowers women and takes care of orphans. In the same way, we have nine ministries in Kenya, which feed people at dumpsites and the internally displaced. We also have other ministries in those countries. The church in the deepest sense is one. So when one part suffers, the whole body is affected. The challenge that believers in Pakistan face is that they are looked at through the lense of their Islamic government. That being the case, it has been difficult to raise funds for our ministry in Pakistan. Yet these brothers and sisters are a vital part of the Body of Christ. Interestingly, when they reported to me they concluded by asking us, "Please claim a great revival for the Christians of Pakistan." They did not ask for money. This prayer was answered. The saints who died in All Saints Church planted the seed of the Gospel. As Tertullian, an African church father, wrote to the emperor, "The more you persecute us the more we will spread; the blood of the martyrs is the seed of the Gospel."

As Christians in Pakistan do, we should look at the glory beyond the cross. We should ask with Paul, "Death, where is your victory? Death, where is your pain?" Christ has conquered death for us. He says, "I am the Resurrection and the Life, he who believes in me will live even though he dies, and whoever lives and believes in me will never die." John 11:25. So for a Christian, physical death is self-defeating, it opens the door for endless life with God. The word of God says this about those who have sold themselves to the devil to kill the righteous ones, "But the fire came down and devoured them. And the devil, who deceived them, was thrown into the lake of fire and brimstone where the beast and the false prophets were, and they were to be tormented day and night forever and ever...This is the second death." Revelation 20: 7-13.

Thus, as Christians we should focus on the victory and the glory. In this regard, our loving Savior says, "In this world, you will have trouble. But take heart! I have overcome the world." John 16: 33.

When we trust in the Lord and abide in Him, not only do we have victory over death, but we also become the springs of water. In the words of our Master, "but whoever receives the water that I give him will never thirst. Indeed, the water I give him will become a spring of water welling up to eternal life." John 4:13.

This water flows to all people, including atheists. The water turns atheists to saints.

The grace of our Lord Jesus Christ be with all the saints.

CHAPTER THIRTY-NINE:
FROM ATHEIST TO A PRAY PARTNER

June 20, 2012

Mary and I were at Rick Husband International Airport, Amarillo, Texas, waiting to board a plane. A lady in her sixties was sitting with her grandson in the row of chairs opposite us. I felt directed by the Spirit to speak with her. We were flying on Southwest Airlines and they do not have assigned seating. You sit wherever there is an available seat. When we were on the plane, Mary found a single seat. The only seat available for me was beside the lady and her grandson. "Where are you heading?" I asked.

"I am going to Houston", she responded. I asked about her occupation and she said she was a homemaker. She asked my profession and I told her that I was a bishop. "Which church?"

"All Nations Christian Church International," I responded, and then asked her whether she attends church.

She said, "I don't attend any church because I don't believe that there is a God." When I asked her why she did not believe she said, "People who go to church are no different from those who do not go church."

"You may be referring to people who attend church but are not true believers." She agreed. "These people don't really define the nature of God. Let me ask you a question, but don't give me the answer. Are you are you left or right handed?"

"Then what is your answer?" she queried.

"You are left handed."

"You are correct. But in our generation children were punished for using their left hand and were not allowed to do anything with their dominant hand."

"Don't you think that the authority figures in your life have influenced your concept of God?" I responded.

We then discussed how the authority figures who punished her for using her left hand contributed to her negative attitude toward the Creator. The situation was made worse by nominal Christians who are without Christ, whom Jesus referred to as weeds, tares, goats, and "five foolish virgins who had lamps without oil."

These are Christians who are devoid of the Holy Spirit and are found in the entire church, from the laity to elders and deacons, and to the entire clerical hierarchy.

We discussed this group of Christians-in-name only. I told the lady that, for me, it would take more energy to try to refute God's presence than to believe in the existence of God. I then shared with her my first encounter with God. "I was six years old when a Being of Light appeared to me. We lived in a mud house and the only interior light we had was from the fire. Every night the fire went out when we went to bed and then the house was extremely dark. One night a Being of Light appeared. I was afraid to look at the Being, so I closed my eyes tightly, but the Being remained visible. I covered my closed eyes with the blanket, but the Being of Light remained visible. I covered my closed eyes with the blanket and the palm of my hands, but I could still see the Being. When I accepted that the Being was in control, the Being vanished and I was left with the peace that surpasses all understanding. The following day, I shared the experience with my childhood friends while we were herding. I asked my friends to close their eyes and look at the sun, so one of my friends did exactly that. I asked him if he could see anything and he said no. I then shared with them my trying to resist looking at the Being of Light but not being successful. "

As I was sharing the story with the woman, the Holy Spirit fell upon her and she committed herself to the Holy Being. After this we had so many things to share. She told me, "When I saw you wearing a cross while we were waiting to board the plane, I heard a voice inside my head telling me, 'That man will sit with you.'" Before we parted I gave her my business card and asked her to remember to pray for me before she went to bed.

A few days later, I got a letter from her in which she talked about God. She discovered that one of His names is Jealousy (we can place no other god before him). She also advised me to read the red letters in the New Testament, because they are actually the words spoken by Jesus. Astonishingly, she narrated a vision she saw as we were talking about God on the aircraft. She saw water that was as clear as the water at the bottom of a waterfall. It was this vision that convinced her of the existence of God. Better still, Jesus Christ revealed Himself to her just as he did with the Samaritan woman, and fulfilled his promise. "Whoever drinks the water that I shall give him will never thirst. But the water that I shall give him will become in him a fountain of water springing up into everlasting life."

Later on the woman shared more about the vision of the waterfall. While the vision convinced her of the existence of God, she also saw that it was connected to something that happened to me when I was a boy. To my utter surprise, this woman was right. When I was seven, we were going to school with another boy who was eleven. Going from Ichichi to Kiruri we had to cross the Maragua River (its name means waterfall). In the middle of the river, I saw trees falling on us. Little did I know we were being engulfed by water. Before we were taken deeper, I saw a beautiful young woman holding my hand. I held the hand of my friend. The young woman took us to the bank of the river. I knew the girl as Waruguru (which translates as "a western woman"), However, it took me sixty-two years to discover that this was an angel. This was unusual because in our area nobody knew how to swim. And this woman could not have had the courage to jump into a surging river except for divine intervention. God had to save my life using a Western lady, so that in time He could use me to win a Western lady to His Kingdom.

It is beyond my comprehension to figure out how God revealed to this woman an episode that took place sixty-three years ago. All we can say is that God is Wholly Other. He has more than a million ways of revealing himself to us. He is a Being who transcends time and space. The Being who shines with unique brightness, stretching over and beyond the cosmos. He is God of all that is, seen and unseen. With His seven eyes, He sees our distant past as if it is today. Our time is in His hand, we are his vassals. He uses us in whichever way He wills. The Holy Being is indeed infinite, incomprehensible and unfathomable, almighty (omnipotent), and all-knowing (omniscient). In the words of the prophet Isaiah: "Do you not know? Have you not heard? The Lord is everlasting God, the creator of the ends of the earth. He will not grow tired or weary, and his understanding no one can fathom. He gives strength to the weary and increases power of the weak." Isaiah 40:28-29.

CHAPTER FORTY:
ACHIEVING IN SPITE OF CRITICISMS

Ezekiel 2:1-7, Psalm 123, 2 Corinthians 12:2-10, Mark 6:1-6

WHAT SHOULD WE DO WHEN we face criticisms? We learn from Jesus that we must continue doing good and retain a positive attitude. When we see the glass half full, the glass will eventually be filled and overflow with blessings. When we see the glass half empty, eventually the water of vitality will evaporate and then the glass is totally dry. We become dry rivers. We become valleys of dry bones.

Instead of becoming vital antioxidants, we become toxic.

Let us learn from Our Lord and Savior Jesus Christ:

Jesus had done great things. He had healed the sick. He had turned water into wine.

He fed five thousand with the picnic lunch of a boy. He taught as no one else had ever taught. He went to his own country. He was where he was born. He taught in the synagogue. Everyone looked at him with mouths half open. They were astonished, they were questioning themselves, "Where did this man get all this? What is the wisdom given to him? See what mighty works are done by his hands! Instead of believing in him, they are belittling him. "We know who he is. We know his brothers, we know his sisters." Then instead of believing in him, they took offense at him.

LEARNING FROM THE STORY

1. Great achievement does not always result in compliments.

There will be some who will be jealous. Put differently, no great deed goes unpunished. There are people who will be offended by what you are, what you have become, and what you have achieved, particularly the religious snobs who are dry wells. But like our Master we must continue to move forward.

We have to keep on doing good. We must focus on the goal.

We have to say with a loud voice, Wacha waseme! Let them speak! We should never view ourselves through the lenses of our critics.

2. Let the criticisms encourage us to excavate our best selves.

Remember your past paradise. Remember an episode(s) when you did great things.

When you were cornered but came out victoriously. This led you to a deep meditation, which resulted in supernatural empowerment. Use those past victories to motivate yourself to face the present challenge. The apostle Paul is reacting to critics by "excavating his authentic self. His opponents are referring to him as "a little bowlegged man." Paul is responding with words. "I don't care what you say."

I know a man in Christ who thirteen years ago was caught up in the third heaven, whether in the body or out of the body, I do not know. God knows. But one thing I remember is that he heard things that cannot be told, which man may not utter." You may try to put this man down! But on behalf of this man I boast.

As with Paul, concentrate on God's strength and your strength. Make the right choice.Keep a positive attitude. We are really our choices and our attitudes.

You may not have control over what people say, but you have control over your choices and attitudes. I fully agree with Billy Riggs that "I fully control the two most important ingredients of a successful and happy life: my attitude and my choices."

Our Master chose to continue doing good works. He marveled at their unbelief, but didn't quit doing what he was doing. But he had to move to another territory. Do not force yourself on the people who cannot receive what you have. Instead move to another territory and continue doing good.

3. The story tells us that he could do no mighty work there.

This tells us that it is those who refuse what you have to offer who are losers.

Jesus did not lose, his countrymen did. He came to his own home but his own people received him not, but as many as received him, he gave them power to be children of God. They abased Him; yet God has highly exalted Him and bestowed on Him the name that is above every name, that at the name of Jesus every knee should bow, in heaven and on earth and under the earth And every tongue shall confess that Jesus Christ is the Lord, to the glory of God the Father.

4. As you keep positive attitudes and make the right choices, lift up your eyes to God.

Whatever is troubling you, commit to God in prayer. When we turn to God, our challenges become steppingstones rather than obstacles. We then hear the Lord talking to us as he did to Paul:

"My grace is sufficient for you, For my power is made perfect in weakness."

Since his power is perfected in weakness, we thrive where we are planted, whether we speak English or Swahili or Spanish. This is particularly true because, as the Apostle John saw, we belong to "a great multitude that no one could count, from every nation, tribe, people and language standing before the throne and in front of the Lamb. They were wearing white robes and were holding palm branches in their hands. And they cried with a loud voice, 'Salvation belongs to our God, who sits on the throne, and to the Lamb.'"

CHAPTER FORTY-ONE:
DO YOU SPEAK ENGLISH?

MY WIFE AND I WERE flying from Houston to Amarillo, Texas. Determined to finish up writing the story of the three eggs, I looked for a spacious seat in the aircraft. Mary was ahead of me. She found a row with an extra seat for me. But I spotted a row with three empty seats, three rows before Mary, at the emergency exit. "There is a seat for you here, darling." She called me three times, but I ignored her because I needed to update the story before we arrived in Amarillo. I knew Mary wanted to visit with me as we flew, but I decided to sit where there were three seats all to myself and I could work on my story. The flight attendant went through his regular chores and came to the emergency exit. Looking at him with a sense of humor, I asked, "But how do you open the door?"

"Can you read?" he asked. Before answering his question, he posed the second question. "Do you speak English?"

"Pocito" (which means "a little" in Spanish) was my reply.

He then shouted at me, "Move away from there!"

"I am just joking, I am a doctor," I responded.

"Even if you are the president, move away from there!" he shouted angrily. I then had to move quickly before he summoned the air marshal who could arrest me as a terrorist. I moved back to sit comfortably with my darling. Now the story of the three eggs had to wait until we arrived in Canyon.

The most aggravating question for those in the diaspora is "Do you speak English?" I have had this question asked three times. The first time I was in Barbados. I had just finished leading the worship that included baptism and preaching. After the service I greeted the people of God. One lady asked me as we were shaking hands, "Dr. Githiga, do you speak English?" Some years later I shared the episode with a friend of mine who was British. Surprisingly, he told me that he was asked the same question in one of the islands in the West Indies. His answer was "We manufactured the language."

The question has a profound meaning for anyone who is eager to give to and draw from all nations. The question is about intercultural experiences and intercultural communication. The question is basically expressing his universe of meaning. For him, the English language is the only one spoken in his parish. More often than not, New Yorkers and residents of other cosmopolitan cities may not ask this question. I have had the blessing of living in three university towns. I have never heard this question asked there.

Those people who have traveled in many countries know that there are as many versions of English as there are nations or tribes. The other continental language I speak is Swahili. I have also learned that each country has its own version of Swahili.

If you are called to minister in another country, you need to bear with the people of your missionary field. Also bear in mind that you will be misunderstood, Know that a familiar word may mean something different to people of different cultures. A story is told of a young woman who was a missionary in Kenya. It took her a long time to gather a group of five girls. This lady opened her first meeting with a prayer and then concluded with "Amen." The word "amen" in the language of these girls meant "I am going to eat you." By the time the young lady opened her eyes, all the girls had fled for their safety.

Thus, as you try to reach out and communicate with people of different cultures, bear in mind that even the familiar words do not mean the same. For an American the word "dog" means a pet which is like a member of the family. For an African it may mean a watchman who should not be let in the house.

Intercultural communication requires that you listen hard, look at facial expressions, and delay your judgment. Do not try to understand it by the first phrase or sentence. Where you do not understand, ask, "What is that supposed to mean?" The more you listen, and the more you stay with people who speak a different version, the more you will be attuned to their language.

When we started ministering to African Americans who had no college education in Sewanee, Tennessee, we had problems of communication. I bought a book on black lexicon to learn their language. It didn't help much. But we started the "each one teach one" Bible study that met in their homes every week. Mary and I became attuned to black dialect. Within one year we had conquered the problem. The first few weeks they had a problem pronouncing my name. One lady took us to a black church and introduced me. "I know he is an African. I know he comes from Kenya. But I cannot figure out his name." The more we ministered with them, the more we loved them and the more they became a part of us. When we were leaving for Kenya, the leading lady asked, "Where shall we get another you?"

When I came back ten years later, I was surprised they remembered all my names and pronounced them well. So, we have to listen to the people who are different from us with patience and love. And eventually, the Spirit will facilitate the communication.

Let us now get the meaning of "Even if you are the president, move!" There is a profound message for all travelers. As a traveler, you need to bear in mind that after 9/11 all travelers became suspects. Traveling in an airplane is not a joke. Flight attendants have a right to tease, but the passengers don't have this right. Thus, the best words that need to come from your mouth are "Yes, sir" or "Yes, ma'am." If you do not need what is being served, just say, "No, thank you."

However, realize that even with good manners, you are not free from humiliation. I shared the above episode with a passenger who sat with me. He said, "I had a worse experience than that. I work with an oil company and travel every week. On one occasion it so happened that the scanner at the security checkpoint detected the residue of gunpowder on my hands. I was searched and interrogated. Then they called my wife to find out whether my story and her story were the same." All this is done for the security of the passages. Nevertheless, this experience should not deter us from traveling. We should trust in God's protection. Pray before you start the journey. Trust in God. Trust his word, particularly Psalm 121 that concludes: "The Lord will keep you from all harm. He will watch over you. The Lord will watch over your coming and going now and forevermore." He will indeed bless the labor of your hands.

CHAPTER FORTY-TWO: THREE SUPERVISORS

God give me work
Till my life shall end.
And life, till my work is done.

ON JULY 16, 2012, I was going to Houston to visit my daughter Rae. But little did I know that this day was designated for spending time with three supervisors. Boarding the plane in Amarillo, I sat with Jason who wore casual clothes. He was astonished when I greeted him. "You look like an executive."

"I am," he gently responded.

"Where are you heading to?"

"I am going to Houston where I am going to interview a candidate who has applied for a job with our company."

"Which company?" I queried.

"I am a supervisor with an oil company."

"What qualities do you look for?"

"I look for people with work ethics and it is difficult to find them in our younger generation. Most people with work ethics are fifty years and older."

"What are the problems with the younger generation?" I asked.

"They want money and a good time, but they don't want to work."

The discussion about employees led to a discussion about China as an emerging economic giant. "What is the secret of their success?" I asked Jason.

"Work ethics," he responded emphatically. We then discussed how work ethics are taught. Jason agreed that the Chinese are harder on their children than Americans.

Later that evening I had further discussions with two other supervisors. They both agreed that work ethics are related to discipline and learning to work at an early age. Joy asserted that her work ethic was instilled by the mother at an early age through discipline. When she was eleven, she was expected to do her chores. Rae, my daughter, started working early in life. If they didn't do what the parent expected, there were repercussions. These preparations made the two young women disciplined workers. Which eventually impressed their employers who promoted them as supervisors. They now enjoy living a middle class life in a middle-class neighborhood.

In my case, I started herding when I was six. At the age of seven I herded sheep and goats and cows. If I let the animals go to the neighbor's farm, I would expect a caning. This of course happened only once. I can still remember the caning as I cried aloud, "Oh my buttocks! Oh my buttocks!" After this I was careful to know where the animals were. I acquired discipline without losing my buttocks. At age ten, I prepared the seedbeds for tea, plums, and cypress trees. As a teenager I had already acquired a work ethic. Work came first. We played after work.

Unfortunately, the American legal system does not encourage children to work. This is perceived as child labor. Thus, children spend most of their time watching TV, playing video games. or watching pornographic material. We need to start training children to work, starting with house chores. Where possible, they need to learn to plant crops and see them germinate and grow. We need to learn to balance between protection and discipline, freedom and control.

Interviewing one of our professors who has lived and worked in China, he contended that the productivity of Chinese society is due to the reverence they give to authority figures. They are united behind and follow the leader. We, of course, cannot recreate Chinese society in America or in any other countries. But we need a balance between child protection and respect for parents and the authority figure.

But it has to be kept in mind that three things mold an individual: parents, society, and self-determination. Parents do not have everything that is required to produce a disciplined person. The government has to create programs that train children for work, or make available programs such as boot camps.

Those who are unable to support themselves need to reciprocate with work for the community. The Bible advises, "He who does not work should not eat."

We have to teach our children the value of work. "A healthy person," Freud asserted, "is the one who can love and work." As mentioned above, my philosophy of life and work is

God give me work
Till my life shall end.
And life, till my work is done.

CHAPTER FORTY-THREE: CONSECRATION OF BISHOPS

SURPRISED BY THE HOLY SPIRIT! This expresses what transpired at the consecration of Tom and Steve. The event was like a delightful carnival. Being a rite of passage, the occasion was preceded by challenges for Tom and Steve, as well as for Mary and me. When we were being afflicted we asked God: "How long, oh Lord?" This is a recurring question for members of the faithful church on earth. There were also experiences that showed God's mercy. On March 5, we experienced untold traveling grace. As we were proceeding to the baggage claim at El Paso Airport, a lady gave us a ride on an electric cart the entire way there, where we found Tom, Sonia, Steve, and Mikah waiting for us.

While we were being jubilant, Doyle and Bill arrived. Tom took us to the Marriot Hotel where we stayed for three days. Besides being in a wonderful facility we were given a fruit basket that expressed love from the Word of Life Church.

On the 6th we had a productive and beneficial retreat. We were surprised to note that besides having the same Spirit, the same faith, the same hope, and the same baptism, we had several connecting threads that made it possible for us to fly high like eagles. Steve and I, although we come from different continents, had many things in common. We both invested in real estate and have the same number of properties. We were both students of London Bible College. Steve came from Aberdare in Wales, I came from Aberdare in Kenya. We both have written songs and published books. Tom has authored several books as well. Tom and I grew up with limited support and limited control, which made us adventurous. This is why although Tom was reared in the Church of God, he willingly accepted God's call to be consecrated in the Anglican tradition. Both Mary and Mikah experienced the challenge of having absentee fathers. Mary's father, a wealthy businessman, was exiled and tortured during the Mau Mau Emergency. He lost all his properties and never recovered. When he came back from exile, he was depressed and died poor. This gave Mary empathetic understanding for the poor and the terminally ill. She has spent many years reaching out to refugees and giving care to the sick and the dying through hospice care. She does this without any salary. Mikah received God's call by seeing footprints that resembled those of her father. She responded to God's call by reaching out to male prostitutes, at her own expense, for four years. She won a good number of them to the Kingdom and a few of them became preachers. Like Doyle and Bill who grew up during the Great Depression, Mary and I grew up in a time of scarcity. In that era, discipline and hard work were the only ways out of poverty. In addition, four of us have ministered in the Cursillo and Kairos prison ministry (this is where we met Doyle). Drawing from these experiences, I am awed by the way God has given us the desire and will for working long hours. We praise him for answering our prayer, which is, "God, give me work till my life shall end. And life, till my work is done." We praise God for using the experiences from our families of origin to prepare us for fulfilling the Great Commission and the Great Promise: "Go therefore and make disciples of all nations."

Matthew 28:19. "…You will receive power when the Holy Spirit comes on you; and you will be my witnesses…to the ends of the earth." Act 1:8.

Consecration, using modern services, commenced on March 7 at 7:00 with joyous and uplifting music. There was a heavy anointing of the Holy Spirit as we followed the liturgy. We really felt the love of God that the Holy Spirit had placed in our hearts. After the consecration the congregation applauded, showing great appreciation for the bishops-elect being entered into the College of Bishops. After a warm welcome, the newest bishops celebrated the Holy Eucharist. We were amazed to note that Tom had been using Anglican ways the same way we do at St. Cyprian's International Church. He used a single cup with the individual Christian dipping the bread in the cup.

As a theologian, I was delighted by the way the consecration of Tom engaged me in theological discourse. One critic who claimed to be an Anglican ecclesiastical authority called me with a question. "Why consecrate someone who is not an Anglican?" Before I could answer the question, the caller concluded, "You are not an Anglican bishop. Were you consecrated by your brother?" In a nutshell, the caller felt he was protecting Anglicanism from Tom and John. Is this possible? The study of the rise and fall of great empires reveals that each empire objectivized and left behind some heritage for the global village. From Sumerians and ancient Egypt we acquired the art of writing, and from Greek empires we inherited democracy and the Greek language, which was used for writing the New Testament and is still used as technical terms in many fields. Religiously, we aquired the Eastern Orthodox church. From the Roman Empire we inherited the art of government administration, road systems (which were useful in spreading the Gospel), and Catholicism. From the British Empire we inherited the English language and Anglicanism.

Once these heritages were objectivized they became available to all the people of God. Thus, neither these empires nor any individual, has the capability of protecting their heritages. To protect Anglicanism from Tom and John is very much like trying to protect the English language from these individuals who already have English names and have written books in the English language. Besides, I have the blessing of being born to Anglican parents and educated in Anglican schools. I was a student in the Anglican theological institutions for seven years, and was an Anglican representative in an ecumenical theological college for five years. I was also ordained a deacon and priest by an Anglican bishop, and was consecrated as a bishop by an Anglican archbishop.

It has to be argued, however, that All Nations Christian Church International draws from three main streams of Christendom: Catholic, Orthodox, and Anglican. Our vestments draw from Roman Catholicism, the titles patriarch and archbishop metropolitan come from our Orthodox heritage, and the Book of Common Prayer comes from the Anglican tradition. We focus on the Holy Spirit. Our vision statement is: "Empowered by the Holy Spirit, we preach the Gospel to all nations." By being in Christ, we bear the fruits of the Holy Spirit that are "love, joy, peace, forbearance, kindness, goodness, faithfulness, gentleness, and self-control. Against such things there is no law." Galatians 5:22-23. We bear the fruit of the Spirit by abiding in Christ who said, "I am the vine; you are the branches. If you remain in me and I in you, you will bear much fruit; apart from me you can do nothing." John 15:5. We are justified in Christ. "Therefore, there is now no condemnation for those who are in Christ Jesus, because through Christ Jesus the law of the Spirit of life set me free from the law of sin and death." Romans 8:1-2.

CHAPTER FORTY-FOUR:
WE GIVE WHAT WE HAVE RECEIVED

MISSION TO THE UNITED KINGDOM AND KENYA,
June 3-July 3, 2014

What do you have that you didn't receive?
I have nothing that I didn't receive.
Fr. Martin and Cynthia Peppiett, my Spiritual parents

The more I reach out to all nations the more I realize that I only give what I have received. In retrospect, I realized that I have received much from many African communities. The East Africa Revival movement, which brought and nurtured me into the Christian faith, is comprised of all tribes in Kenya. My spiritual and professional parents include Hungarians, Dutchmen, Australians, the British, Canadians, and Americans. As the Bible emphatically states: "To him who received more, more is required." The intension of the mission journey to the United Kingdom and Kenya was to visit the people of God from whom I have received so much, including the Church in Kenya. I am most grateful to God who gave me the desire of my heart. The Holy Trinity also accorded me unspeakable traveling grace.

I boarded United Airlines in Houston on June 3, 2014, and landed at Heathrow airport on June 4, where I was cordially welcomed by the lady in uniform with the gracious words "Welcome, darling." This set the tone to the hospitality and love I experienced in the Living Faith Diocese. Bishop Steve and Mama Mikah took great care of me. Ian our driver took us to places we had planned to visit. My desire was to visit headquarters and the people who have made enormous contributions to what I have and what I am. We visited the Boys Brigade Headquarters who helped us when we were starting the First Nakuru Company of Boys and Girls Brigade. That became the mother of all brigade movements in Kenya organized by Anglican, Presbyterian,and Methodist churches. Mary became the captain of the Girls Brigade (GB) and I was captain of the Boys Brigade (BB). The BB motto, which impacted our character, is "Sure and steadfast." The GB motto is "Seek and follow Christ." We spent quality time with Steven Dickenson, brigade secretary, and was overjoyed when Bishop Steve decided to start a BB and GB company in his diocese. This is a great program for youth and I would strongly recommend our churches to start this program. For more information visit www.brigade.org.uk.

In addition we visited Oxfam headquarters, the body of Christ that helped me when I was reaching out to the troubled children and youth in Nakuru, Kenya. They assisted in putting up the first buildings of the St. Nicholas' children home.

The most rewarding time was a visit with Father Martin and Mama Cynthia Peppiett who are my spiritual parents and guardian angels. Martin was my vicar and mentor when I was a young evangelist at Nakuru. They ministered to me after I had nasal surgery. My beloved Africans could not leave me alone. The more I was visited and talked, the more I bled. African Christians stayed with me. They of course drew from African ontology: "I am because we are, and since I am, therefore we are."

I don't know how Father Martin knew that I was just about to bleed to death. He came and took me to his guest house, where I stayed for two weeks until I was completely healed. If they had not given me a refuge you wouldn't be reading this message. When I was visiting with them, they gave me the number of Canon Captain Charles Dickens, who was my principal at Church Arm College, Nairobi. I was surprised to converse with him in Swahili. Better still, Father Martin gave me a biography of Bishop Neville Langford-Smith, who ordained me deacon and priest and was a celebrant at our wedding. After reading the biography, I had a great appreciation for Bishop Neville and the Church Missionary Society, which sent him to Kenya. Neville was the only European bishop in Kenya. From him I learned how to be "the only." During my ministry in the United States, I was the only African priest," which was both a blessing and a challenge.

The Ministry with Living Faith Church was awesome. This ministry was established by Bishop Steve Evans, whom we consecrated in Patriarch Cathedral in El Paso, Texas. The membership of the church includes fifteen nations. It is truly "All Nations!" They have maintained unity in diversity, which is a core value of Anglicanism. They worshiped in Spirit.

They have a team of well-organized evangelists who preach the good news in streets and institutions.

On June 10, I boarded Brussels Airlines at Manchester with Dr Davis, and we were in Nairobi the following day. We were met by Archbishop-elect William who was chief organizer of our mission. He took us to Saba Saba, where we held the first clergy conference on June 12-13. The hundred clergy and spouses in attendance were very receptive with a give and take attitude. They gave Dr. Martin and me Kenya Gospels DVDs and handwoven handbags for Mary and Sara. On June 15, we ministered two churches at Ichichi, my birthplace. The liturgy in both churches was very spirited. They indeed worshipped in Spirit and truth. We felt the presence of God just as we had in the Living Faith Church.

On June 17, we journeyed to the Great Rift Valley. On June18-20, we had a clergy/spouses conference in Nakuru, Mary's birthplace, and where I was ordained a priest, ministered to the troubled children, and planted a church in the 1960s. The conference, which took place at All Nations Church, was coordinated by Rev. Gordon and Mary Onyango. Gordon was raised at St. Nicholas's Childrens Home, which we established with the aid from Oxfam. Our music team was St. Nicholas' Harmony, our children. They have been ranked as the best gospel team in the country. The conference was crowned by the ordination of Gordon and Mary. As at Saba Saba, the clergy were very receptive and hospitable. They gave me a Kikuyu Bible. Interestingly, I didn't have a Kikuyu Bible even though Kikuyu is my mother tongue.

On June 19, Bishop Thomas Gwako and his five-year-old, Joy, came for us at Nakuru and we drove to Kisii. The following two days we had two crusades in Kisii, and on both occasions the spirit was high and we were well received. At Ogembo twelve children committed themselves to Christ.

On the 23rd we left for Nakuru, but Father Martin and William left for Nairobi so that Martin might fly on the 24th. Canon Habel and I were in Nakuru visiting with families and friends, and ministering with Gordon and Mary. On Saturday, Gordon and Mary took me to the dumpsite where we started the ministry of troubled children in 1965. There we found pigs, birds, and people salvaging through the garbage, and small shelters for the homeless. Hilton Church, which was planted and is being ministered by Gordon and Mary, was in this neighborhood. On Sunday morning, we had the regular service with Mary leading the music while Gordon was leading the service. Both were wearing chasubles, which were graciously donated by Archdeacon Joe and Mama Marlene Cordero. We felt the presence of the Holy Spirit in the worship. In the afternoon, we had a marriage enrichment seminar, which was attended by Christians from several churches. We discussed the challenges that were facing marriage partners today and the secrets of success in marriage. There was a very high degree of participation. The event was crowned with a love offering for the patriarch, which amounted to 955 Kenya shillings. This was a generous contribution from the church at the dumpsite. May the Lord richly bless them.

To the end, we experienced amazing grace, love, hospitality, and the presence of the Holy Spirit, which is in keeping with the words of our Master, "God is Spirit, and his worshippers must worship him in spirit and in truth, for they are a kind of worshippers the Father seeks." John 4:23. As noted above I learned that I could only give that which I have received. Christians of many nations and tribes have planted seeds in me and thereby prepared me to minister to All Nations. I still remember the last sermon which I heard from Peppiatt in the 1960s: "By love serve one another." When I visited them this summer, he read this message: "I pray…that all of them may be one, Father, just as you and I are one, for you are in me and I in you. May they also be in us so that the world may believe that you sent me. I have given them the glory that you have given me, that they may be one as we are one." John 17:21-23.

This is indeed our prayer for all Christians of all nations.

CHAPTER FORTY-FIVE:
I DREAMED I CARRIED AN ELEPHANT

On November 29, 2014, I had a big dream. I saw myself carrying an elephant in what appeared to be an arena with spectators. I was amazed that I was not exhausted. I then woke and found that it was a dream.

Puzzled with the unusual dream, I asked my son Isaac, as we were driving to a Pizza Hut, if he would interpret the dream for me, and advise me on how I can ride on the elephant's back, rather than carry the elephant on my back. It so happened that he was attending a mandatory staff meeting, and having worked as a manager of a bigger restaurant, he knew the problem, but didn't want to be a know-it-all. So he told me he was planning to behave like a monkey and for that reason "it is difficult for a monkey to interpret the dream." After this, I called my old friend Professor Francis Githieya, who comes from our ethnic group. He revealed to me that the dream had a message about my mission to India. He compared the Kenyan elephant to the Indian elephant. "Kenya elephants are bigger and untamed, so you cannot be on their backs. Indian elephants are smaller and tamed, so they will carry you." He also told me that hunters of tigers ride elephants to safeguard them from the tigers. He reminded me of a Kikuyu proverb, "The elephant is capable of bearing its tusks." (Njogu ndiremagwo ni muguongo wayo). Also in my community we have a saying, "Nothing is an elephant", when we are facing the most challenging undertaking. It is similar to the Biblical saying, "Nothing is impossible with God."

This is what I sing most of the time:

There is nothing too hard for thee, dear Lord
There is nothing too hard for thee.
Nothing! Nothing!
There is nothing too hard for thee.

The image of the elephant captured the undertaking I was facing at that time, what I was planning to do, and what I had to face in the most challenging month of December. A day before the dream, my "to do" list included communicating with eighteen pastors and bishops around the globe about the position of education coordinator and with several accreditation bodies about the accreditation of our university, I was preparing two books for publication and was talking with three publishers. Being a tent maker as St. Paul was, I was negotiating with mortgage companies for a better interest rate for our rental properties, and planning the overseas mission for 2015, including missions to India and Kenya. Professor Francis' comparison of Kenyan elephants with Indian elephants was relevant to what I was facing, and the great expectations of the people preparing the missions. The Indian planner was more realistic. One of the planners in Kenya had so overpriced the cost of the Church Leadership Conference that I had resolved to discontinue dealing with him.

As it was with the Wise Men and Joseph who were warned by the Lord through dreams, the dream was warning me to get the elephant off my back. It was putting me into a receptive mode. I was prepared by three episodes. One came when I was in a grocery store and heard an Anglo uttering a Swahili word. I jokingly asked, "Did I hear someone speaking Swahili?"

"I just said mambo jambo," was the reply.

"Did you know the word 'jambo' is a Swahili word for 'Hi?'"

From there I decided to walk in Westgate Mall. After the walk I sat at the food court and ordered a glass of lemonade to sip as I read a book from Free Grace on the *Deity of Christ* that I am now receiving free from Free Grace. I was, indeed, riding an elephant.

An Indian touched my hand and said, "Jambo."

"Jambo," I responded. I now had a second Pentecostal experience. After small talk with the Indian, I went on reading the *Deity of Christ*. I was being empowered! I was again interrupted by another Anglo with a question.

"Are you a pastor?"

"How did you know?" I queried.

"You look like a pastor."

"I am."

He said, "I am a Salvation Army pastor."

This was quite interesting since I didn't have either a clerical collar or a cross. I felt affirmed by God, as He affirmed Jesus, "This is my beloved Son, of whom I am well pleased." In the case of Jesus, after the affirmation he was led by the Spirit into the wilderness. The part I was interested in is, "And the Angels ministered unto Him." I prayed that the Spirit would lead Mary and me where we will be ministered to by angels. So I called my nephew Isaac Methu in California and told him that we would like to be with them for a week. He graciously accepted and advised us to bring walking shoes.

Gracious Father accorded us inexpressible traveling grace. Through the security check, we were told that we didn't need to remove our jackets, shoes, or even belts. We didn't have to raise our hands to go through the scanner, a requirement that gave the terrorists a feeling of victory, for their intention is for all travelers,

including senior citizens, be treated as suspects. As we were coming back through Ontario airport, the security officer sang ""Happy birthday to you" for Mary.

Five days with Methus' family was indeed a sabbatical rest. We stayed in a motel, where we did nothing but rest. We didn't even have to make the beds. Breakfast started at 6:00 a.m. and was served until

11:00 a.m. This allowed us to sleep late. With my nephews and their families, we walked in a mall, a modern time cosmic center where humanity is nourished by humans. Beyond our expectation, we had lunch in a rainforest, which was peopled with animals. We sat beside the elephant. The Way wanted to reinstate the vision of the elephant. We appeared so small in comparison to the biggest living land mammal the Lord had created. It reminded me of the words of St. Paul, "I can do all things through Christ who strengthens me." And our Lord's encouraging words, "With God, all things are possible."

Relaxing and sharing the meal with Methu's family was a sanctification of life. Included in the family was my cousin, Isaac's mother, who is ninety-three years old with a good memory. We shared the story of my grandfather's family. He had sixteen wives, my grandmother being the youngest. Remembering our large family was a celebration of life. The challenges which most of us faced and overcame assured us that God was with us then, is the one who is with us, and will be with us tomorrow. He is the one Who was, Who is, and Who is to come.

On Sunday we worshiped in Kingdom Interdenominational Community Church, which had begun in Methu's home. Now it is a big church ministered by two pastors, both with doctorates in theology. The music was uplifting, the message encouraging. Mary and I were called to greet the congregation, and then sang for them in Swahili Psalm 23, which has been encouraging us for the past 46 years. We were overjoyed to meet Dr. Peter Mwiti and Esther. Dr. Mwiti was my student from St. Paul's University, and so dear to me for being a successful student and specializing in my field.

After church we had lunch with Isaac's mother and sisters and their families. I was awed by the intermarriages in my cousin's family. So we enjoyed the meal and fellowship with many nations. This fulfilled my joy as the father of many nations.

As we shared the meals and conversation with Methu's family, I was astonished to note that we had many related experiences, which included challenges and blessings that we faced when we were in courtship. Elizabeth, who comes from Taita, one of the smallest communities in Kenya, faced challenges for dating a Kikuyu, who comes from the largest community. She stood her ground and stuck to Isaac for better or for worse. In my case, I was challenged by my family for dating a city girl. Being a young, dedicated diocesan employee, the challenge came from my bishop. It was reported to my father in God that I was dating an immature girl (Mary was just turning 18) and my beloved bishop stepped in by stopping our plans for marriage and transferring me from Nakuru to Eldoret—a hundred miles away. As I later learned from his missionary colleague, he did it so that the love between Mary and me might grow cold. After this, my father in God, who was a missionary from Australia, took a three-month vacation and left behind thoughts of Mary and me. Being also a church army officer, I was visited by the general secretary, Captain John Ball, who warned me about the course I had taken. But the more hurdles we faced, the more we loved each other, and the more we remained faithful to God.

When the bishop returned from his vacation, the very first thing I did was to visit him and tell him that I still loved Mary. We had a good ending in that the bishop gave us his blessing and agreed to be the celebrant of our marriage. As we were discussing these episodes, we learned that God allowed these obstacles to be in our way to strengthen our marriage. Interestingly, when Mary and I were facing these challenges, I was strengthened by Elizabeth's father, Mshila, who I visited with a college mate, Benhard Mshila. He made the statement, "Human beings can delay, but have no power of preventing God's will from being done." He supported his argument with Israel's flight from Egypt.

So if you are facing challenges, if you remain faithful to God, God's will will be done. If you are planning to do great things for God, be assured that no one can prevent God's will from being done.

If you are facing an elephant, know that God is the one who created the elephant. If God calls you for an overseas mission, obey Him and you will be surprised by what He will do through you. Fascinatingly, I was enlightened by the words in a cup that was presented to me several years ago by my great niece, Marga, who is Mshila's great-granddaughter:

TO ACCOMPLISH GREAT THINGS,
WE MUST NOT ONLY ACT,
BUT ALSO DREAM.
NOT ONLY PLAN,
BUT ALSO BELIEVE.

While we must believe that there is "nothing elephant" in the eyes of God, four things are necessary: dream, plan, believe, and act. Five things are also valid: vision, courage, creativity, self-confidence, and self-control. VISION is the ability to see what others do not. COURAGE is the ability to act despite fear. CREATIVITY is the ability to think outside the box. SELF-CONFIDENCE is the ability to withstand criticism. SELF-CONTROL is the ability to delay gratification.

A visit with Prof. Peter and Esther Mwiti was energizing. Esther had prepared a delicious meal. The spirit was high and we experienced the love of God. The most rewarding were the memories of our time together at St. Paul's University in the 1980s when Peter was my student. Peter is my joy and crown for following in my footsteps. He specialized in my field and has written books on counseling. He teaches in two theological institutions and counsels.

Sharing St. Paul's University memories was rewarding. To my great surprise, Esther informed us he still remembers the license plate of the teacher's car in detail, but cannot remember the details of her present car. Surprisingly, I have always asked, "How come I still remember I had a Ford Escort KIA, but cannot remember the name of our present two vehicles? Did the automobile driven by the teacher seem that much different from our current vehicles? I remember my car was used for medical emergencies. If a student got sick during the night, I was called to rush him to the hospital, and we might stay until 2:00 a.m. But at 8:00 a.m. I had to be in the class teaching. Our salaries were so minimal that we didn't have enough money to buy gas to drive to Nairobi. To portray the best image to the student, we had to drive to Limuru, which was 8 miles, leave our car there, and board the bus.

Why we cannot recall a few letters and numbers, I have no answer. After finding this a common experience, I made the effort to memorize the registration plates of our Subaru and Honda Accord, which at this writing I have not succeeded in doing. The answer to this question will come from my students. Suffice it to say, our fellowship together with the Mwitis was very energizing.

Staying with the Methus gave us a good rest. They gave us many presents, more than we ever expected. As Isaac was taking us from the motel to the airport, he squeezed more gifts into our bags. This really fulfilled our desire of receiving, rather than giving. By the time we arrived in Canyon, our batteries were fully recharged.

The following day, which was December 24, the loving Father advised us to continue enjoying the Sabbath rest. No carrying or wrestling with the elephant. On Christmas Eve, we attended a beautiful Christmas service led by the Rev. Deborah Huffman of First Christian Church in Canyon. These lovely Christians housed our university, and regard Mary and me as a part of their family. On Christmas Day, Mary, Isaac, and I enjoyed ourselves.

The big lesson here for bishops, archbishops, cardinals, patriarchs, and popes is: You don't have to be a major actor on Christmas and other high seasons of the Church. Remember that you are a sheep, and the Great Shepherd can nourish you through the people of God. Said differently, you don't have to always carry the elephant.

However, remember to share your dream with the people of God. I shared the dream of carrying an elephant with Seminary students and my church. During the evening of Christmas Day, I listened to a message on my cell phone. There was the voice of Marcos Shalala from Nubia Mountain. He was inviting me to a Nubian community Christmas celebration. I was sorry to have missed the event. When I later visited with Marcos, he told me that he was carrying an elephant. He had been working very hard to bring the Nubian in Amarillo together.

On this Christmas Day he had succeeded, but it was like carrying an elephant. Twenty-five families attended: twenty-one were Muslims and three were Christians. This, indeed, was an elephant. He wanted his teacher to see him carrying an elephant.

God can employ the image of an elephant when he calls us for a great undertaking. This may include physical suffering. St. Paul was knocked down and for three days he could not see, eat, or drink. Isaiah wrote how God spoke to him, "For the Lord thus spoke to me with a strong hand upon me and warned me not to walk on the way of these people. Isaiah 8:11.

He said, Go and say to these people:
Hear and hear, but do not understand;
See and see, but do not perceive,
Make the hearts of this people fat,
And their ears heavy, and shut their eyes
Lest they see with their eyes,
And hear with their ears
And understand with their hearts
And turn to be healed.
Isaiah 6:9-10

The Lord of Host calls us to face the elephant. Some calls are preceded by intensive suffering. KTN interviewed a lady pastor whose call came after an agonizing experience. Early on the morning of her wedding day, she was raped by three men who stabbed her and left her broken and dying. When the police came, they couldn't find a pulse, so she was taken to the city mortuary. There they heard her coughing and realized she was alive, and took her to the hospital. When she healed, she planned what she called her "second wedding." On the night of their wedding, they felt cold and brought charcoal fire to warm their bedroom. Tragically, she lost her bridegroom through carbon monoxide poisoning. Her third wedding was successful. The unspeakable suffering led her to ministry. She is a wounded healer.

If you are facing an elephant, you need to find out whether God is allowing difficulty to come your way to get your attention. Share what you are experiencing with your spiritual director or a prayer partner. When Samuel was called by God, he went to Eli. He thought Eli was calling him. When he was called the third time, Eli understood that it was God who was calling the boy, so he advised the boy to say, "Speak Lord, for thy servant hears." When God called the fourth time, Samuel responded as he was advised by Eli.

A spiritual director is very useful in our spiritual pilgrimage and ministry. He helps us to know when to say, "Speak Lord, for thy servant hears." The interpretation of a dream is important both in political and spiritual leadership. Joseph became the second man in Egypt by interpreting Pharaoh's dream. He helped the world to survive seven years of hunger by his ability to discern the meaning in a dream. Daniel became second in command in Nebuchadnezzar's kingdom by interpreting a dream. Professor Francis Githieya had the same insight, as you will see in the following pages.

My friend, the Venerable Dr. Martin Davis, who is the ANCCI international liaison, and a professor of systematic theology, was my companion. We had planned a mission to India but God, who is omniscient, revealed that our mission would be to Sri Lanka, where one of the tourist entertainments is to cross the river on the back of an elephant. We would also see elephants walking with people.

God foresaw that Martin and I would minister in a Bible Church in that country. The vision of carrying the elephant without being tired was predicting our experience in this lovely country on the coast of the Indian Ocean. Interestingly, Martin had seen an elephant in his dream. Martin was riding an elephant but "Nothing was going well," unlike my dream in which I was carrying an elephant. God was revealing to him the difficult choices that we had to make in Chennai, India, and Colombo, Sri Lanka. They were choices between greater evil and lesser evil.

The words that highlighted our mission to India are in Mark l: 12-13. "At once the Spirit sent Him to the desert and He was in the desert for forty days, being tempted by Satan. He was with wild animals and angels attended Him."

Mark puts in a nutshell Jesus' experience in the wilderness, and what Martin and I went through during our mission. Interestingly, our mission coincided with the celebration of Lent, Jesus' forty days in the desert. Surprisingly, the layover and flying time from Dallas to Chennai was 40 hours, marked with an abundance of grace and maximum challenges. There were wild animals, angels, and Satan. However, there were more angels than demons. On boarding Air Canada in Dallas, a young lady who was to sit next to me volunteered to put my carry-on in the overhead bin for me. And when I was going through security in Toronto, an officer asked me whether I was coming from West Africa. "I came from the United States," I responded. Had I come from West Africa, I could not go through Canada. I felt kinship with brothers and sisters in West Africa who have been ostracized by the global village because of the deadly Ebola virus.

In Frankfort, Germany, I asked the agent for directions to the gate where I had to board Lufthansa Airline. With great honor and appreciation, she took me all the way to the gate. After being in the air for nearly twenty hours, we arrived in Chennai, India. Fighting jetlag, as we were going through customs, we saw a big signboard with the words, "VISA ON ARRIVAL." Contrarily, we were informed that we could get an entry visa to India only in Sri Lanka at the Colombo airport. We were then led to a transit lodge and locked in. The second problem occurred when we were not allowed to purchase our tickets to Colombo. The man who locked us in had to purchase the tickets for us. He asked for our passports and credit cards. As the Kikuyu proverb puts it, "When the bull is knocked down it has no power to resist being marked with a hot iron." So we had to choose between the lesser evil of surrendering our passports and credit cards to a stranger, or being lock in forever. We, along with another American researcher, complied. We endured three agonizing hours as we waited for the tickets, passports, and credit cards. Our fourth inmate, a flight attendant from Sri Lanka, told us what we SHOULD NOT HAVE DONE. "You shouldn't have given him your credit cards and passports. You should have asked him to use his telephone and purchased the tickets over the phone." I felt butterflies in my stomach, or as a Kikuyu would put it, "I had water in the stomach." After the three agonizing hours the officer appeared, like an angel. We stayed in the lodge and slept sitting up the whole night. At one point I got thirsty and the lady inmate gave me a quarter gallon of apple juice. She also gave us useful advice about the Sri Lankans, "Be very careful. Those people can rip you off."

At 2:45 pm we boarded Air India for Colombo. We were surprised we were given entry visas to Sri Lanka. We were told that we could not get an Indian visa at the airport. Since it was Friday evening, we could get it on Monday. So, we took a taxi to the Ramada Hotel, which was close to the Indian Embassy. To our great surprise, the door to ministry was opened through our housekeeper, Pradeep. When he saw our crosses, he showed us great respect and told us he belonged to two churches, a Catholic and a Bible Church. Pradeep knelt down whenever he visited us. He made our rooms twice a day, and gave us extra bottles of water. We asked him if he would introduce us to his pastor, who delightedly invited us to be guest preachers on Sunday. On Sunday, Pradeep first took us to his home. His wife, who appeared to be very godly, greeted us with great honor. His children greeted us by kneeling and touching our shoes. We were seeing the humility of Christ in these children. I taught them a chorus,

There is nothing too hard for Thee, dear Lord.
Nothing, nothing, there is nothing too hard for Thee.

As I have noted, I like singing this chorus whenever I am facing an elephant. I was also preparing these angels for the time they will face an elephant.

After the visit we went to the church where we were warmly welcomed by the pastor. The service started with praise and worship, followed by our sermons. After the sermons, we had to pray and lay hands on each of the ninety Christians. All the children kneeled and touched our shoes. We experienced amazing love. We realized this is where God wanted us to minister. Returning to the hotel, Pradeep came in the evening to ask if we had had dinner. We told him that we were planning to eat a chocolate bar. He said, "No, you need to eat something." He took us to McDonald's and bought hamburgers for us. We experienced the compassion and generosity of God through Pradeep, who had a limited income. We now enjoyed being on the back of the elephant.

On Monday we took a taxi to the Indian Embassy. The agent directed us to another location. There we were directed to another office for photos. And there we were informed that it would take seven days to get a visa. From another source we learned that seven days may turn into seven weeks. We quickly decided to return to the United States. We had to buy tickets that we had not budgeted for. So on February 24, we boarded Sri Lankan Airlines to Dubai, then Air France to Paris and Atlanta, and then Delta Airline took us to Dallas. Martin and I parted in Dallas and finally I flew with Southwest Airlines to Amarillo.

Being a student and a researcher by passion, I did extensive research on the political system in India. I found that European and American church leaders who were attending Christian conferences were denied entry visas. In the same month, two Catholic Archbishops who were to attend a liturgy conference were denied visas. Catholic News reported, "As Church leaders protested a rising tide of anti-Christian sentiment, and Indian government added new fuel to the protests by denying visas to two Vatican officials who had been scheduled to address a conference on liturgy next week." Archbishop Arthur Roche, the secretary of the Congregation for Divine Worship, and Archbishop Portase Rugambwa, the president of the Pontifical Missions, quickly cancelled plans for a visit to India after learning that they would not be granted visas. A spokesman for the Indian Bishop's conference said their bishops would press government officials for an explanation." However, we learned that the Indian government doesn't owe you any explanation when it comes to denial and cancellation of visas. In our case, we were being killed with kindness. Sri Lanka was a dumpsite for unwanted Christian leaders.

We further learned that in India Christians are being persecuted by both extremist Hindus and Muslims. Acts of violence against Christians include arson, re-conversion of Christians to Hinduism by force, threats of physical violence, distribution of threatening literature, burning of Bibles, raping of nuns, murder of Christian priests, and the destruction of Christian schools, colleges, and cemeteries. This girl, for instance, was burned for being a Christian.

And thus, by being locked in transit detention and being dumped in Sri Lanka at our expense, we were getting a tiny dose of what the saints are going through. We praise God for counting us worthy to suffer with the Indian saints. I can now claim, "I am John, your brother and companion in suffering for the kingdom with patient endurance that is ours in Christ Jesus." The words, which I got from our brothers and sisters, were very encouraging: "I can do all things through Christ who strengthens me." This includes being crucified with Him, so that we may rise with him. We were reassured by his victorious presence: "Fear not, for I have redeemed you. You are mine. When you go through the waters, I will be with you... When you walk through fire you will not be burned. For I am The Lord your God, the Holy One of Israel, your Savior." Isaiah 43:1-5. I like the way St. Paul writes about the effect of elephants in his life as he faithfully ministered for the Lord; "But we have this treasure in jars of clay to show that all-surpassing power is from God and not from us. We are hard pressed on every side, but not crushed, perplexed, but not in despair, persecuted, but not abandoned, struck down, but not destroyed."

We always carry in our body the death of Jesus, so that the life of Jesus may also be revealed in our body." 2 Corinthians 4:7-10. We were convinced that whatever happened will not diminish God's love for one another. In the words of St. Paul, "I am convinced that neither death nor life, neither angels nor demons, neither the present nor the future, nor any powers, neither height nor depth, nor anything in all creation will be able to separate us from the Love of God which is ours in Christ Jesus."

And to all those who are persecuting Christians, I would warn you with the words of the third century African church father, Tertullian, "The more you persecute us the more we will spread, for the blood of martyrs is the seed of the Gospel."

To all who are going through tribulation because of their faith in Christ, remember what the Bible exhorts us: "If we die with Christ; we shall also be raised with him." This good news is for our loved ones and we who have died in Christ. The Bible tells us: "Brothers and sisters we do not want you to be ignorant about those who fall asleep, or to be grieved like the lesst of men, who have no hope. We believe that Jesus died and rose again and so we believe that God will bring with Jesus those who have fallen asleep in him. According to the Lord's own word, we who are still alive, who are left until the coming of the Lord, will certainly not precede those who have fallen asleep. For the Lord will come down from heaven, with a loud command, with the voice of the archangel and with the trumpet call of God. And the dead in Christ will rise first. After that we who are still alive and are left will be caught up together with them in the clouds to meet the Lord in the air." 1 Thessalonian 4:13-17.

CHAPTER FORTY-SIX:
THE ASCENSION OF CHRIST

They were looking intently to the sky as He was going. When suddenly two men dressed in white stood beside them. 'Men of Galilee,' they said, 'why do you stand here looking into the sky? This same Jesus, which you have seen taken from you into heaven, will come back the same way you have seen him go into heaven.'

ACTS 1:10-11

THE BIBLE INFORMS US THAT Jesus Christ ascended into heaven, how He will descend the sky in his second coming, what we should be and do as we await his coming from God, and who is on the throne in heaven.

In his second coming, we will see him as he was seen when he was ascending. Luke writes, "He will come in the same way as you seen him go into heaven". The Second Advent differs from the first in that every eye will see him. Revelation puts it this way: "Look, he is coming with the cloud, and every eye will see him, even those who pierced him." Revelation 1:7.

We should not set the date of his coming. Jehovah Witnesses set a date in 1944, and when he did not appear, they lied, saying he came and went to his glory. His message to the disciples before he ascended was: "It is not for you to know the time or the date the Father has set by his authority." Acts 1:7. In Mark 13:31, Jesus tells us that even the angels do not know the hour: "No one knows about that day or hour, not even the angels in heaven, nor the Son, but only the Father."

What should we be and do? Jesus makes it crystal clear: "But you shall receive power, when the Holy Spirit has come upon you, and you shall be my witnesses in Jerusalem, in Judea, Samaria and to the end of the earth." I believe this is the greatest promise because it was fulfilled forty days after Jesus gave the promise. What is awesome to me is that for the fifty-seven years that I have walked with Christ, there has never been a day when I asked God for the infilling of the Holy Spirit without getting an immediate answer. When the Spirit comes in our hearts, we are empowered for the ministry. We become witnesses, ready to bear the cross. We can tell those who persecute us, "It does not matter what you are going to do with my body, as long as I have breath in my mouth I will never stop claiming Jesus as my Lord and Savior." As noted, in my recent research on persecution in India, I found a photo of an eleven-year-old girl who was burned for refusing to deny Christ. This reminded me of a song which was composed by an Indian girl who was facing the same challenge:

I have decided to follow Jesus,
No turning back, no turning back.

These witnesses are able to do that through the dynamic power of the Holy Spirit. So my dear brothers and sisters, no matter what you are facing, you are a victor. Know that greater is He who is in you than the one who is in your persecutors. To fuel the fire of the Holy Spirit recite Psalm 47:

1 Clap your hands, all you peoples;
Shout to God with a cry of joy.
2 For the Lord Most High is to be feared;

He is the great King over all the earth.

3 He subdues the peoples under us,

And the nations under our feet

4 Sing praises to God, sing praises;

Sing praises to our King, sing praises.

5 God reigns over the nations;

God sits upon his holy throne.

6 The rulers of the earth belong to God,

And he is highly exalted.

Amen. Come, Lord Jesus.

We are victors. The Risen Lord put it this way: "To him who overcomes and does my will to the end, I will give him authority over the nations." Revelation 2:26. Better still, those who overcome are part of "…a great multitude that no one could count, from every nation, tribe, people and language, stood before the throne and in front of the Lamb…wearing white robes and holding palm branches in their hands. They cried out with the loud voice:

Salvation belongs to our God,
Who sits on the throne,
And the Lamb.
Revelation 7:9-10

CHAPTER FORTY-SEVEN:
MESSAGES FROM THE NATIONS

BISHOP STEPHEN, THE PHILIPPINES:

Dearest Patriarch +++John,

Since the month of July this year we already have started the Regular Bible Studies in some homes, most especially the new ones, and those who invited us to do Home Bible Studies. Soon, I will make a schedule of training for the people who would like to be used by the LORD in doing Home Bible Studies. I have already done the editing of the POWER OF THREE- THE DISCIPLESHIP & EVANGELISM MANUAL, I will have this photocopied and then start training people on how to use it more effectively.

The Director of the PAROLE & PROBATION OFFICE called me up for a meeting, because she would like us to be involved in making a follow-up of those who have been paroled under probation, and not only those who have been paroled, but would include their families. I am planning to use the POWER OF THREE here also.

We were given a chance again to visit the Camp of the MORO NATIONAL LIBERATION FRONT (MNLF) Muslim Rebels Camp, together with some Government Officials, Military, and NGO'S we were there to celebrate with them Eid'l Ft'r, and of course, the Government brought 100 sacks of rice, 20 carabaos, vegetable seeds, fertilizers, and there was also a program where I was one of the main speakers. We also participated in the Edi'el Ft'r the last day of the RAMADAN where the Muslims in our area gathered in one place and requested me to be one of the SPEAKERS, well, some people/ministers do not like the idea of accepting the invitation because to them accepting such an invitation is a compromise, but what is a compromise? To me, I did not compromise my faith, what I shared and preached is JESUS CHRIST, is that a compromise? I shared and preached the JESUS in the BIBLE. I believe that even Muslims need JESUS, they need to hear the GOSPEL OF CHRIST which is the GOSPEL OF PEACE.

August 10, 2014- my 56th Birthday the Church Members surprised me by what they had prepared for me. They prepared testimonies, gifts, and they brought something for lunch. We had Lunch Fellowship and my son Fr. Adrian prayed for me, and together with the brethren laid hands on me. Then we were requested to do the Feeding Program to a school where most of the students are Muslims, there were about 400 children. We were again escorted by some military men, in fact, the military helped us in serving the children.

Our Feeding Program at the Dumpsite is doing well. Sometimes we cannot use the Gym because the Village has another activities which take priority. I will make another report for that.

PRAYER REQUESTS:

1.) Please continue to pray that the LORD will make it possible for us to own this area/place we are using as our dwelling and a Worship Center because most of the Children of the owner are in Canada already, there is only one left here in Iligan City and his family is working for their papers. I don't know how could this be possible, but I only believe that GOD has HIS own way of doing things and in providing us what we do really need.

2.) Please pray that we can be able to reach our goal of 200 Worshippers, by the end of this year.

3.) Please pray that the LORD will bless our effort in doing HOME BIBLE STUDIES every night.

4.) Please pray that we can be able to publish the EVANGELISM & DISCIPLESHIP MANUAL- THE POWER OF THREE. Anyway, I will start by photocopying it and have the book bound, this is what we are going to do at the moment.

5.) Please pray that the LORD will help us open an ANCCI SHORT TERM BIBLE TRAINING CENTER, for those who would like to serve the LORD in the Fulltime Ministry. This is by the month of June 2015.

6.) Please pray that the LORD will continue to provide for us the ceiling of the Worship Center, we still need woods, nails and for the labor of the Carpenter.

7.) Please pray that there will be openings for Church Outreaches this year.

8.) Please continue to pray for our Feeding Program at the Dumpsite, and that the LORD will also open other depressed areas in the City as He provides us the Feeding Program.

9.) Please pray for us as we think and plan for the Livelihood of the mothers at the Dumpsite, as well as the women in the Church.

10.) Please pray for us too, and for all of our Priests at ANCCI Philippines, that GOD will continue to provide us our daily needs for our families.

May the LORD bless you richly and keep you real good.

Agape,

+Stephen and Sonia+

FROM KISI, KENYA

Hi,

Bishop John,

I received the present you sent through our Bishop William.

He is a Godly man who sent me Kenyan shillings 8,300 which is one hundred dollars. Bishop, we thank you and may our God bless you and give you more. Kindly, send me the email of Bishop Matara.

Pastor Zachariah Matoke.

Kenya.

I hope your plan to Kenya it is well my friend we are doing fine with the work of God. I hope the proposal which I gave, I think you are working with it the school are doing fine with the children, but I think I told you about the two classes we have the shortage of the class in our school so many orphans as you know are there which we supporting that is why we are having some shortage of classrooms. So we need your prayer from you. Thank you greet all of your friends tell them that we love them.

Yours Bishop John Nyabuto

CRISIS IN PHILIPPINES.

We are mourning with our brothers in the Philippines because of the devastating typhoon. I have contacted our two ministers: Rolando Aboloc of Tribal Ministries and Remegio Blanco of Harvester Ministries. Blanco was unable to respond, possibly because of the network. And this is what Brother Roland wrote:

Dearest beloved Bishop John & Family, I am just taking a chance to reach you in this email address because we don't know where to go this time of crisis. We are in the Island of Visayas now the second major

Island of the Philippines, but please if you will send help do not use my address because I cannot receive it. This place is a ghost town already no more business, no stores, no hotels, no Banks, no Offices, and thousands of people are in exodus to other places." Any financial assistance will be greatly appreciated.

FROM PAKISTAN

Dear Papa John.

Greetings!

First of all I am very thankful to God that you are absolutely fine by the grace of God, I am always blessed when I receive your e-mails, I found my papa in you. I also thank you for sending money for the "Children Bible School". I am serving these children by faith and I will continue it until the end of my breath. We are continuously praying for you and your family,

Please keep us in your prayers too.

With Lots of Love,

Your Daughter,

Evangelist. Monica Najeeb.

From India

"Our children were praying for the Bible. Bishop John sent $50 for me and my Family, but we decided to buy the Bibles for the children. Praise the Lord," Rachel

"Our three children were not attending the school because we had no money for tuition, Bishop John sent us $50. We praise the Lord because now our children are in school". Peter (We were visiting Rachel and Peter when we were refused visas and detained in the Chennai airport. When we were talking about how to finance the clergy conference, Rachel wrote, "Financially, I am very, very poor." Yet you can see her selfless love with the children.

From Kisi, Kenya

Dear Bishop John, Thank you so much for financial aid, we have used the money to buy food for the children in the orphanage. Bishop Matara

Nakuru, Kenya: Dad, thank you so much for your financial help. Pastor Gordon

As you can see from these messages, Mary and I have the amazing blessing of being spiritual parents of so many children from many countries. We also have enormous challenges since nearly all our bishops, clergy, and evangelists receive very small stipends from their ministries. Nearly all of them are "tent makers," a phrase used for those ministers who employ Paul's model of ministry. They are full-time in other occupations and full-time in ministry. They also follow in our footsteps. Our business is rental properties. And Mary is employed full time in a retirement home. Yet miraculously, the Spirit of the Lord has brought to us over one thousand ministries operating in over seventy countries. Surprisingly, we do not have employed office staffs. All our ministers and evangelists do their regular jobs full time and serve God full time.

From Philippines, Triba Ministries

Dear Pastor Bishop John & family,

It is very seldom in my life I use computer and never that I interfere Pastor Rolando' email address but it is sad to say that I brought Pastor Rolando to Hospital last night because he suffered High Blood stroke he is unconscious and admitted in the intensive care unit.

I want to keep it myself and not to tell anyone I don't know where to go and what to do but to trust God in this time of crisis because I am shy and afraid I might be misinterpreted, because all you have done to help us in our work here in the Philippines. But I just cannot afford not to tell you what happened. In the family it is Pastor Rolando provides our daily subsistence though how very busy he is in the Ministry, he is a good father husband and a servant of God.

I am just a mere wife helping him in the work of God I don't know what to do this time that he is in hospital there are many prescription of Medicine, and medical treatment required to save him from imminent Danger

I cannot think of anything but God, and I am writing you to let you know and to humbly ask your personally a compassionate help of finances to unload burden for medical expenses, I am sorry I should not have done this, because I don't want to be misinterpreted of taking advantage but this time I need to ask your help. Please I am asking your generous help in this time of my family crisis. Thank you very much. Sister Belen S. Aboloc

Dear Sister Belen,

We are so sorry to hear about the sickness of Pastor Rolando. This is a great challenge to you since he is the communicator. We are praying for both of you that you may be strengthened, that he may be healed, and that the Lord may provide for medical expenses.

++John

Dearest Beloved Pastor Bishop John I am very happy because of your email I felt unloaded with problems and felt the presence of the Lord because of your encouragement and your prayers Yes this is my name you can use to send some help thank you very much I know God will multiply to you and will abound the works of your hands.

Sister Belen Aboloc

Dear Bishop John & family,

Thank you very much for the money you sent to us. This is a great help to us in this time of crisis I believe that God will shower you with all of his abundant blessing. Thank you very much.

Sister Belen Aboloc

As you can see from these messages, Mary and I have the amazing blessing of being spiritual parents of so many children from many countries. We also have enormous challenges since nearly all our bishops, clergy, and evangelists receive very small stipends from their ministries. Nearly all of them are "tent makers," a phrase used for those ministers who employ Paul's model of ministry. They are full-time in other occupations and full-time in ministry. They also follow in our footsteps. Our business is rental properties. And Mary is employed full time in a retirement home. Yet miraculously, the Spirit of the Lord has brought to us over one thousand ministries operating in over seventy countries. Surprisingly, we do not have employed office staffs. All our ministers and evangelists do their regular jobs full time and serve God full time.

CHAPTER FORTY-EIGHT:
FOR OUR LEARNING

IN THE PRECEDING CHAPTERS I have shared my blessings and challenges in the ministry. The following pages are intended to shed some light on the faithful ministers and parishioners. It is my delight to encourage all those who are called to fight a good fight of faith. It is for those who believe that they are called to bear the cross and wear the crown. It is for those who are intentionally waiting for the bridegroom with the oil in their lamps.

When you are going through fire, you need to realize you are not alone. The Apostle Paul put it this way: "No temptation has overtaken you except such as is common to man: but God is faithful, who will not allow you to be tempted beyond what you are able, but with temptation He will make away to escape, that you may be able to bear it." I Corinthians 10:13.

Do realize that what you are going through, what someone else has gone through? At one occasion after losing the pulpit due to a prophetic message, I met a Methodist minister who was very much interested in knowing where I came from originally. I told him that I come from Kenya. "Where in Kenya?" he asked.

"In a village known as Ichichi," I responded.

"I have been there," he responded with great joy. But to my surprise I learned that he too had lost his pulpit for the prophetic message, but God has called him to a more fulfilling ministry.

So whatever you are going through for your faithfulness and obedience to God's will, there is someone else who has gone through it. Be assured that God will hold you in the palm of his hand. You will make it! And it will leave you a better person. As the Swahili proverb put it, Kilicho na mwanzo kina mwisho. Whatever has a beginning has an end.

THE PROPHET'S REWARD

My pastoral theology professor at Vanderbilt University made a great remark in this regard, "If you are a true prophet you must be ready to be treated as one." One of the greatest gifts of the prophet is a joyous relationship with God, a relationship that makes him a mouthpiece of God. They experience the love of God firsthand. They enjoy the peace of God that transcends all understanding. They delight in having the knowledge of the secret of God and seeing the events before they occur. They enjoy foretelling and forth telling the will of God. Yet both Old Testament and New Testament prophets suffered for their messages. They were afflicted by unregenerated religious and political leaders, particularly when they were told what they did not want to hear.

Jeremiah is one of the prophets who suffered terribly at the hands of his fellow priests and prophets, and the kings. During the reign of Jehoiakim, Jeremiah was commanded by the Lord to go to the temple and deliver God's message to the prophets and priests. He was ordered by God, "Do not diminish a word." When he prophesied as he was commanded, he was seized by the priests and the false prophets, saying, "You shall surely die!" They took him to the king to be put to death. But he was rescued through divine intervention. See Jeremiah 26.

If God has called you to be both a priest and a prophet, you experience great psychological pain when your fellow priests afflict you.

When this happens, think of Jeremiah. You need to bear in mind that the enemy's objective is to remove you from the church. In this case, remember that the visible church comprises wheat and tares, sheep and goats, five wise virgins and five foolish virgins, children of darkness and children of the light. You need therefore to stay connected with the children of light. Immerse yourself in the Spirit. Follow the footsteps of great men of God like Jeremiah and St. Stephen. Draw heavily from the Universal Power. This is exactly what Stephen did. Luke tells us, "And Stephen was full of faith and power, did great wonders and signs among the people." The greatest wonder took place when he was being stoned for his testimony. Luke narrates: "But he [Stephen] being full of the Holy Spirit, gazed into heaven and saw the glory of God, And Jesus standing at the right hand of God. And said: 'I see heaven open and the Son of God standing at the right hand of God. As they were stoning him his last words were: Lord Jesus receive my spirit, Lord do not charge them with this sin.'" Acts 6:8-7:60.

So whatever you are going through, keep on gazing to heaven to the Lord of hosts. Know that you have a special relationship with a loving Father who is always in control and has your best interest at heart. Realize that you have a High Priest who is sitting at the right hand of God who went through what you are going through. Are you being afflicted by ecclesiastical authority or a lay pope? Remember your Lord went through it. Are you condemned to death in "Jerusalem?" This happened to Jesus.

He once lamented, "O Jerusalem, Jerusalem, the one who killed the prophets and stoned those who are sent to her! I wanted to gather your children together, as the hen gathers her chickens under her wings, but you were not willing! See! Your house is desolate: for I say to you, you shall see me no more till you say, 'Blessed is he who comes in the name of the Lord.'" Matthew 23:39.

Whatever you are going through, cultivate peace and joy. The joy of the Lord is your strength. My most cherished saints are Samuel and

Sarah Muhoro, who were students of my father. Their dreadful episode occurred in the dark and cold night. The persecutors broke into their home and demanded that they deny Christ. When they refused, the killers started butchering Samuel. Sarah was so filled with peace and joy she started smiling. The killers stopped killing the husband and then cut Sarah's small finger and rebuked her, "Why are you smiling at us! Don't you know that we are murderers?"

"I know," Sarah responded, "but God loves you."

So Sarah's peaceful demeanor diffused their anger. They stop killing Samuel but took all the blankets. Sarah said to them as they were leaving, "Folks! Don't forget we have children. We need some blankets." They then threw some blankets to them and said, "Be praying for us."

As a prophet of the Most High, remember his encouraging words: "Be still and know that I am God." Psalm 46:10.

"Cast your burden upon the Lord and He will sustain you." Psalm 55:22. Own the great promises. Remember the words of our precious Savior, "Blessed are you when they revile you and persecute you, and say all kinds of evil against you falsely for my sake. Rejoice and be exceedingly glad for great is your reward in heaven, for so they persecuted the prophets who were before you." Matthew 5:11-12.

YOU ARE WRESTLING WITH UNREGENERATES AND BACKSLIDERS

Do you understand that you are wrestling with unregenerates or backsliders? These are people who are at the church but are not in the church. They have form, but no substance. They are Christian by name and formality, but have locked the Spirit of God out of their lives. They are with the people who are in the Kingdom of God, but they are not in the Kingdom and cannot see the Kingdom of God. They are very much like unconverted Nicodemus. You remember the story. When he went to Jesus by night and started praising Jesus. Jesus told him the truth about himself and about the Kingdom of God. Jesus emphatically told Nicodemus, "Most assuredly, I say to you unless one is born again, he cannot see the kingdom of God."

So do realize that your flock includes sheep (the born-again) and wolves. You have wolves in all church strata from lay reader to archbishop. But you also have the children of light in all church positions. We understand the mind-set of both groups because we were all born in sin. The apostle Paul put it this way, "For we ourselves were also foolish, disobedient, deceived, serving various lusts and pleasures, living in malice and envy, hateful and hating one another. But when the kindness of the love of God our Savior toward man appeared, not by work of righteousness which we have done, but according to his mercy: he saved us, through the washing of regeneration and renewing of the Holy Spirit, whom he poured out on us abundantly through Jesus Christ our Savior. That having been justified by his grace we should become heirs according to the hope of eternal life. Titus 3:3-7. Here Paul is calling a spade a spade. If you are going through it this time, you may discover that all those who are waging war with you are in the same basket. They are deceivers and deceived. On one occasion, the person who falsely accused me to the ecclesiastical authority had been challenged by the sermon I had delivered about regeneration. I still remember the anointing I had on that Sunday, which was following by Episcopal visitation. This lady lied and said that I was Africanizing them. After this she was so tortured by her conscience she called me the following day and said, "Father, forgive me for lying to the bishop about you. I have a clean heart but a dirty mouth."

My answer was, "Could you please pick up the phone and tell the bishop that you lied to him?"

She responded, "I don't have the courage to do that."

Then the following day I found a gift in my office from my accuser. But my dear bishop was more interested in lies than truth. He so regarded the lie as absolute truth that he laid off the only black priest he had in the diocese to save his flock from "African-ness and accent." The underlying issue was unregeneration.

If you are in Spirit, you have no problem distinguishing the unregenerated from generated. The life of a slave to sin is characterized by foolishness, disobedience, deception, lust, malice, envy, hatred, anger, and jealousy. The regenerated bear the fruit of the spirit, which are love, joy, peace, long suffering, kindness, goodness, faithfulness, gentleness, and self-control. J.C. Ryle, one of the most spiritual Anglican bishops, wrote about eight marks of the new birth.

The first mark of the new birth is whoever is born of God doth not commit sin.

"Whosoever is born of God sinneth not." 1 John 5:18. This according to Ryle this means "He no longer takes a light and cool and easy way to sin...He hates it and abhors it, and desires to cut off it's roots and branches with his whole heart and mind and soul and strength."

2. The second mark is faith in Christ.

Whoever believes that Jesus is the Christ is born of God. 1 John 5:1.

Ryle states, "I do not mean by this a general, vague sort of faith which the devil possesses. I mean rather that (conviction) which comes over a man when he is really convinced of his own guilt and unworthiness and sees that Christ alone can be his Savior." I should admit that I have never seen someone who is in Christ waging war with the faithful minister of the Gospel. So those who do are thorns in the flesh, "Christians without Christ." They are a part of our mission field and this is why we have to forgive them because tomorrow they may be convinced by the Spirit of their sins.

3. The third mark of the new birth is holiness.

The apostle John tells us that everyone who practices righteousness is born of Him. He who is born of God keeps him, and the wicked one does not touch him. I John 2:29, 5:18. Those who are in Christ are not led by the devil but by the Spirit of God. They therefore work with but not against the priest.

4. The fourth mark of the new birth is spiritual mindedness.

Since they are risen with Christ they "seek those things which are above." They set their affection on things that are above, not on the things that are on earth. These lovely Christians have no desire to complain about the pastor because he is earning more money than they. They couldn't care less about a typographic error in the bulletin. They may be liturgical, but they don't worship the liturgy.

5. The fifth mark of the new birth is victory over the world.

For whoever is born of God overcomes the world. And this is the victory that has overcome the world, our faith. Ryle put it this way, "The spiritual man is no longer like a dead fish floating with the stream of earthly opinion; he is ever pressing upwards, looking unto Jesus in spite of all opposition. He has overcome the world." So whatever you are going through, remember that you are a winner. Own God's great promises: "Fear not, I have redeemed you; I have called you by name, you are mine. When you pass through the waters I will be with you; and through the rivers they will not overflow you. When you walk through the fire, you shall not be burned, nor shall the flame scorch you. For I am the Lord your God, the Holy one of Israel, your Savior." Isaiah 43:1b-2. So if God is for us who can be against us? In all things we are more than conquerors through Him who loved us. We are indeed winners.

6. The sixth mark of the new birth is meekness.

Remember it is by pride that the angels fell and became devils. Some of the people who are antagonistic to the priest were people who had seen the light. But when God exalted them, they reciprocated with pride and became autocratic. This was what happened to Saul, the first king of Israel. He started well, but eventually he fell out of grace and became ruthless to the very people who were fighting for him, including his son Jonathan, and David his son-in-law. Some of the church leaders were elected by the people of God because of their grace and fruitful ministry. But when they acquired money and power, they became corrupt and empty wells.

If you have gone through it, you will agree with me that the people who belittled you were arrogant. But when you are going through it, connect with meek people. You will find in the church family those who are humble and are more concerned about repenting of their own sin than in projecting them to their spiritual leader. These people have no time to find fault with others or be a busybody about their neighbors. Most clergy will tell you that the very first person who came to them when they arrived in the parish was also the very person who started poisoning the body of Christ against the minister.

7. The seventh mark of the new birth is a great delight in all means of grace.

I still remember what happened to me when I committed myself to Christ at the age of 15. Things which never mattered became most important: church worship, Bible study, Christian fellowship, and volunteering for anything that the priest asked me to do. Being in the company of the people of God became as sweet as honey. As a newborn baby, I had a great desire for the sincere milk of the Word. Those who are born again have a give and take attitude. They draw the best from the clergy and the church family. When they come to church, they are interested in particles of gold rather than sand. They will always find something that will draw them closer to God. They attend church services and special events regularly. They can benefit spiritually from the gathering of two or three as they can from five thousand. This is why you, as a priest, must value their presence even if they may be one or two. Remember that they don't worship numbers, but God. Like David they will tell you: "The law that you give means more to me than all the money in the world." Psalm 119:72 (GNB).

8. The eighth mark of the new birth is love toward others.

As the Apostle John admonishes: "Beloved, let us love one another, for love is of God, and everyone who loves is born of God and knows God. Those who give you a hard time in ministry are also people who have locked God outside of their lives. And the message that they need is that which Jesus gave to Nicodemus: "Unless one is born of water and the Spirit he cannot enter the Kingdom of God." Don't be discouraged, however, if you don't succeed in winning them for Christ. Remember Jesus, who is God-man, had Judas for three years. And Judas chose the way of damnation. So you are just a messenger. You are not a messiah.

IT IS WAR BETWEEN LIGHT AND DARKENESS

Being regenerated means that you are a bearer of Christ. You are Christopher. You abide in the one who said, "I am the light of the world, He who follows me will not walk in darkness but have the light of life." You are a child of God in a special way. You are saved. David would put it this way: "The Lord is my light and my salvation, whom shall I fear?"

By being the bearer of light, you scare the children of darkness. When you scare them, they hate you. The light in you scares them because their deeds are evil.

Being a child of light implies doing things in a right way and in God's way. You follow the footsteps of your Master who said, "I am the way, and the truth and life." You take a higher way that enables you to operate in a higher energy system. You possess the keys to success: forgiving, giving, and thanksgiving. You are also fully convinced that the **will of God** will never take you where the **grace of God** will not protect you.

This high energy system does not allow negative emotions such as jealousy and fear. Children of darkness, on the other hand, are dominated by a lower frequency system of negativity, which "suck up the energy." This has a negative effect on their activities. This will turn them to a "C" or "F" while you are an "A" in your performance. This provokes their jealousy and gives them the desire to destroy you. If you are suffering for being a child of light, don't put your light under the bushel. Keep on shining. Remember the word of the Apostle John, "In Him was life, and that life was the light of men and the light shines in the darkness and the darkness has not overcome it." You are not a victim, you are a victor. In the deepest sense the darkness is the absence of God. It is absence of Universal Energy. But as a child of God you possess this enormous energy. It was this energy that broke the chain that had bound Peter in prison and forced the prison doors open. It is the same light that guided the Israelites in the wilderness. It was the same light that guided the Wise Men to the baby Jesus. And it is the same light that will lead you to your eternal home. When you select nonphysical light, you see things through the authentically empowered rank in creation. You then have more ability to see without obstruction, more ability to live in love and wisdom, and more ability and desire to help others to see and experience the light. The light will lead you to a realm where you will experience perfect peace, perfect love, and perfect joy.

Made in the USA
San Bernardino, CA
16 June 2016